Matters

What is Policing?

Policing Matters

What is Policing?

P A J Waddington
Martin Wright

LearningMatters

First published in 2010 by Learning Matters Ltd

British Library Cataloguing in Publication Data
A CIP record for this book is available from the British Library.

ISBN: 978 1 84445 355 9

Cover and text design by Toucan Graphic Design Ltd.
Project Management by Diana Chambers
Typeset by Kelly Winter
Printed and bound in Great Britain by TJ International Ltd, Padstow, Cornwall

Learning Matters Ltd
33 Southernhay East
Exeter EX1 1NX
Tel: 01392 215560
info@learningmatters.co.uk
www.learningmatters.co.uk

All weblinks and web addresses in the book have been carefully checked prior to publication, but for up-to-date information please visit the Learning Matters website, www.learningmatters.co.uk.

FSC
Mixed Sources
Product group from well-managed
forests and other controlled sources
Cert no. SGS-COC-2482
www.fsc.org
© 1996 Forest Stewardship Council

Contents

1   Why a policing degree?

The purpose of the book

This book is aimed at all those higher education students who are taking degree-level *vocational* courses in policing. It is important to draw attention to the vocational aspect of these degrees, for there are many courses available that study policing as an object of inquiry, usually as part of criminology and criminal justice courses. The approach of these latter courses is to examine policing, much as one might examine parliamentary democracy – that is, as an important institution that deserves scrutiny in order find out and critique how it works. That knowledge is only tangentially related to being a good and effective police officer, just as studying parliamentary democracy is unlikely to get you elected as a Member of Parliament. The approach of this series is quite different: we are in the business of producing a new generation of *professional* police officers. This book and others in the series aim to provide skills and knowledge that will not only facilitate entry to the police, but also provide a sound foundation for a professional policing career. This involves learning a great deal, but also acquiring habits of mind – scepticism, rigour, respect for reason and evidence – that will become increasingly relevant during the twenty-first century. This entails abandoning some misleading, but popular, beliefs about policing, as well as learning what might be uncomfortable truths. However, we would be sad if, at the end of this book, you did not feel inspired to forge a career in policing!

A word of welcome

Welcome to this book and the series of which it forms a part. Welcome also to your degree-level course in policing. Finally, welcome to the commencement of your policing career. Make no mistake, your *career* begins once you arrive at your university. It may even commence once you make it known that you have applied for, let alone been accepted on to, your university course. You will notice that others tend to treat you differently once they learn of your ambitions, but this is just the beginning, because as a police officer (which you aspire to become) you will be set apart from the remainder of the population. Police officers (as this book will demonstrate) have onerous responsibilities and enormous powers to coerce their fellow citizens. Staff and students will expect more of you, as a policing student, than they will of other students. You will be expected to behave more responsibly and conscientiously. If you fail to do so and behave generally like most students, others will look aghast and exclaim, 'And them, *policing* students as well! We'd have expected better of them!!!' Get used to it! Policing is as much a matter of *character* as it is of intellect. This is not to say that intellectual demands on a policing degree are fewer than on other courses. Instead, it means that, *in addition* to the stringent intellectual demands that will be made upon you, there will also be a test of character. In short, a policing degree is not a soft option; it is among the hardest ways to earn a degree. So, the question you have to answer is, 'Are you tough enough to do this?'

When you have decided that you are, read on.

A *policing* degree?

Almost all policing degrees are offered in collaboration with one or more police forces, with whom those developing the degree will have collaborated prior to its formal validation, and usually the respective police force will offer work placements of some kind for students on the degree course. Some policing degrees are only available to students who are already serving police officers. So, why do so many police forces throughout the UK believe that it is desirable for their officers to have a degree? The answer is provided by Her Majesty's Inspectorate of Constabulary who, in 2002, carried out a 'Thematic Inspection of Police Training'. The subsequent report stated:

> If the Service is to be viewed as a profession, the initial training and development provided must be comparable with other professions and, in particular, those within the criminal justice system. The sum total of formal training which a probationer receives is around 31 weeks out of the 104-week probationary period. No other profession within this system would allow new staff to practise after so little training or without the achievement of a recognised qualification.

(HMIC, 2002, para. 4.2)

That report estimated that, on the first day of patrolling, a police officer needs to be familiar with 5,000 pieces of legislation. That's right, 5,000! But that is not all: police officers need to be knowledgeable about all of the following.

- Case law made on a daily basis by judges sitting in the highest courts of the land making decisions about how statutes passed by Parliament should be interpreted and what constitutes an offence under Common Law (the unwritten law that has been passed down by previous generations).

- Using protective equipment appropriately.

- Providing first aid to those who have been injured.

- Distinguishing between people who are agitated and aggressive because they are intoxicated; because they are diabetic and suffering from an insulin overdose; or because they are mentally ill or emotionally disturbed; as well as taking appropriate action as needed.

- Recognising as victims those who have been traumatised by a crime they have witnessed.

- Appreciating cultural diversity that might influence how closely you stand to another person or how firmly you shake their hand.

- Actively engaging with all those in an area who can influence behaviour and forming partnerships with them to address local problems.

- Identifying recurring problems that might be symptoms of a deeper malaise; researching that problem to find solutions to it; persuading others to play their part in applying the solution; and evaluating its success.

- And much else besides.

This is, to put it mildly, a demanding job description and yet those recruited as officers receive only sparse training in the very basics of the work. Previous generations of officers have jealously guarded the value of 'on-the-job' training and with good reason, because it is only by experiencing some of the realities of policing that you, or anyone else, will come to understand what is required. You will experience life as you never knew it: squalor that leaves you wondering whether this country is truly a part of the developed world; depravity on a scale you never imagined; duplicity honed to precision by people for whom this is their sole social skill; dead bodies aplenty (some of them partially devoured by pets driven mad by starvation); oh yes, and criminals who will swear black is white even when the contrary is plainly in view!

Valuable – indeed indispensable – as experience is, it is not all there is to being an effective police officer in modern Britain. Public expectations have never been higher and the knowledge required has never been so esoteric. The professionalisation of policing is long overdue and, as a student on a policing degree, you will be a pioneer in this process. There are many advantages to pioneering, not least the chance to take your pick of oppor-tunities, but there are costs too – fear and distrust among those who do not share your advantages. Managing that fear and distrust is also a test of character. Wear your professionalism lightly, but never shed it!

Professionalisation of the police is a 20-year project, which will only be complete when all recruits have qualifications similar to those you aspire to obtain at the conclusion of your course. An all-graduate profession is better than nothing, but will not attain pro-fessionalisation. That relies on the recruitment of people who have acquired, through dedicated study and deep reflection on their work placement, an in-depth appreciation of their work, and an ability and desire to challenge established practices and become agents of transformation. For policing in Britain, as elsewhere, remains largely as it was conceived in the nineteenth century, but the society that is policed has changed enormously. It is vital that a new generation of police officers can recognise what should remain constant in policing and what should change; what is myth and what is reality; what is desirable and what is dangerous. This is why professional police officers must retain intellectual curiosity throughout their careers, and intellectual curiosity is the most valuable skill that you will acquire during your degree studies.

A career in policing can be enormously challenging and fulfilling; to a policing student who is committed to a professional police career, it offers abundant opportunities. To a policing student who is committed to a professional career, it offers the prospect of making a difference to the world in which we live.

A policing *degree*?

Why must professionalisation rely upon vocational degree-level courses in universities? It was to provide vocational degrees that the vast majority of universities were founded, even the most eminent. At first, universities educated the priesthood, and then medicine increasingly required a university education. The burgeoning industrialisation of the nineteenth century provided a hunger for engineers and others with specialist knowledge. Increasingly, as the British economy became a knowledge economy, that demand has spread to new occupations that rely upon information technology. The growth of welfare occupations led to a similar revolution in the status of teachers, nurses and social workers. Just as one would not wish to be treated by an unqualified physician or nurse, educated by a teacher without a professional training, or counselled by an unqualified social worker, so it is becoming increasingly anomalous for a police officer to lack an equivalent qualification.

Those with established professional status inevitably look askance at occupations struggling to establish themselves in the pantheon of the professions. So it is inevitable that those devising such degrees will strive to ensure that a degree in policing is *equally, if not more,* intellectually demanding than any other degree offered by their university. Just as your character will be tested during your degree course, so too will be your intellect. There is plenty of scope for intellectual rigour in policing degrees, because the police role is so diverse. What use, one might ask, is a police public order commander who does not have a firm grasp of crowd psychology and the politics of protest? What use is a police investigator who does not understand how forensic scientists collect and process materials at crime scenes so as to produce good evidence? What use is a sergeant who has never considered the management of people very deeply? What use are police officers who do not appreciate cultural diversity in the society that they must deal with on a daily basis? This only skims the surface, but highlights the wide range of academic disciplines that have direct relevance to building a professional police service. No one can claim to cover it all – a policing degree is only the *beginning* of a professional police career, but should be a sound foundation for future learning. Different universities will emphasise those aspects of the police role that reflect their mix of expertise, so the diligent student should evaluate each degree and choose that which best engages their attention.

Not everyone who takes a policing degree will become a police officer. As we will discuss in Chapter 8, the concept of policing embraces more than the police themselves. Apart from police forces, there is an army of investigators and security guardians employed by central and local government. These range from the exotica of the secret security service to the more mundane, but nonetheless valuable, investigators of social security or tax fraud. In addition, for every sworn police officer there are at least two or three private security operatives who perform functions very similar to those of the police. However, not everyone will continue into a career associated with policing for a wide variety of personal reasons. They should rest assured that vocational degrees, especially those as demanding as policing degrees, are favoured by employers who appreciate the intellectual demands and tests of character that are involved.

The purpose and structure of this book

The series of which this book is the first to be published aims to support degree courses that seek to provide a foundation for a professional career in policing. The task this book aims to perform is the excavation of the foundations into which others can pour concrete knowledge and skills. Excavation is an apt metaphor because we aim in this book to dig beneath the surface of mythology that surrounds policing and challenge popular misconceptions. We hope also to open up new ways of imagining policing and recognising the challenges that exist in the police role and lie ahead. We will frankly consider some of the dangers that also lie ahead for the police recruit – dangers that do not lurk on the streets, but in ways that police have traditionally responded to the complexities of their role. Finally, we look beyond the police organisation to others who contribute to the maintenance of law and order, appraising not only the positive contribution that should be recognised and harnessed, but also the problems that surround partnership with those whose mission it is to maintain order.

Learning features

This book is interactive – not intended simply to be read, but used to stimulate activities and discussions among students, whether in class or outside. There are case studies drawing attention to specific examples relevant to the text; and tasks in which you should engage in order to get the most out of the text.

The main aim of the book is to encourage reflection – to prompt you to consider how you would deal with situations and what you would feel about them. Another aim is to appraise how the police currently deal with those situations and how this may be improved. At this stage of your career you may or may not have begun work as a police officer, special constable or Police Community Support Officer, but once you do you should continue to reflect on the issues. Above all, this book should challenge how you regard policing. If you conclude that it simply confirms what you already knew, this book will have failed. Challenging your assumptions is not intended to be comfortable, but will help you to begin the process of becoming a fully professional police officer.

REFERENCES

Her Majesty's Inspectorate of Constabulary (2002) *Training Matters*. London: HMIC.

2 Introduction: law and order

CHAPTER OBJECTIVES

By the end of this chapter you should be able to:

- recognise how media representation of crime and policing distorts reality;
- have a more realistic understanding of crime;
- understand its relationship to policing;
- appreciate the limitations and weaknesses of the view of policing as 'crimefighting'.

Introduction

The police officer is such a familiar figure in daily life and such a staple of fiction that many of you may imagine that you know exactly what the police do. The police prevent crime, enforce the law and detect offenders by picking their way through the thickets of evidence, pursuing leads and possessing an unerring sixth sense for unmasking the criminal. Criminals are wily, devious and knowledgeable about how to exploit their rights to defeat the ends of justice, while victims are unblemished paragons of virtue in need of protection. Criminologists have discovered what is called the 'law of opposites' (Surette, 1998), which is that more or less everything that appears in the media about crime is not only wrong, but the *opposite* of the truth. The police spend only a minority of their time on crime-related activity, criminals overwhelmingly suffer mental difficulties of various sorts or are addicted to substances, and often it is difficult to distinguish between offenders and their victims.

As a student on a vocational policing degree it is vital that you begin with a realistic understanding of what the police do and do not do – an understanding rooted in firm evidence and not reliant on mass media distortion. That is what this book aims to provide, but first we must repudiate some common media-inspired myths. Worse still is the way that the police conspire with the media to propagate distortions. We shall return to this later when we discuss police culture.

Crime and disorder

According to the most recent Home Office figures, in 2007–08 there were a little over five million crimes committed in England and Wales. That bold figure seems alarming to the public and a considerable challenge to a police force of around 140,000 officers. However, crime is not as you might imagine it. The Home Office figures highlight some fascinating aspects of the crime problem.

Offences known to the police

There are two quite different sources of information about crime and disorder. The most established is the record of offences known to the police from which the figure of five million crimes is taken. What the phrase 'offences known to the police' refers to is a rather complex legal and bureaucratic process. It begins with someone believing that a crime has been committed and feeling sufficiently aggrieved to report the matter to the police.

Crime is a *legal category*, but ordinary people do not often distinguish between wrongdoing and criminality. Yet, some wrongs are dealt with by the civil, rather than criminal, courts and justice systems. It is wrong to take payment and not deliver the goods for which it was made, but that is more likely to be a civil matter regarding the contract entered into to supply the goods, rather than a criminal issue of theft. To establish that someone has committed a crime entails that the case can be proven beyond 'a reasonable doubt', whereas civil wrongs are determined on the 'balance of probabilities'. Some common wrongs can be both criminal and civil.

Even if something is crime, it would depend upon how it is defined. For instance, in 2009 the issue of assisted suicide became a cause célèbre after Debbie Purdy, who has multiple sclerosis, sought clarification of the law and received support from the House of Lords (which was the final court of appeal before being replaced by the Supreme Court), who invited the Director of Public Prosecutions (DPP) to consider issuing guidance on how the law should be interpreted. This effectively decriminalised assisted suicide in certain types of cases. Some people still consider it wrong to help someone commit suicide, but in some instances covered by the DPP's guidance it will no longer be treated by the prosecuting authorities as a crime.

Not everyone who is afflicted by what they firmly know to be a crime goes to the lengths of reporting it for a variety of reasons, the most common being that the offence was insufficiently serious to take the time and trouble needed to report it.

Vandalised windshield wipers

Leaving my car in a public car park while having a convivial evening with friends, I returned just before midnight to find that someone had bent the windshield wipers and car aerial, so that they were now entirely useless.

I went to the local police station, across the other side of town, which took me 15 minutes or so. Upon arrival I waited in a lengthy queue for my turn. I was surrounded by drunks and people nursing wounds and grievances. One man vomited in the corner and the stench filled the room.

Eventually, I reached the counter and spoke to the official behind the counter. I told her my story and she typed the details on to the computer. She then asked for my driving documents, which I had neglected to bring with me because I had not envisaged that I would need them. So, I was issued with a form requiring me to produce them within a stipulated time. I returned home at around 2.30 a.m.

The following day I obtained replacement windshield wipers and radio aerial. I ferreted through the documents relating to my car and eventually found everything. I dutifully returned to the station, stood in a queue (thankfully vomit-free) and proffered my documents to the official behind the window. The round trip took approximately an hour and a half and cost a couple of quid.

I vowed never to report a crime again, unless I could not avoid it!

A 14-year-old girl, accompanied by her mother, arrives at the police station to complain of being raped.

The mother explains that earlier in the day her daughter awoke feeling ill. She took her daughter to the doctor, who informed her that her daughter was pregnant. The daughter explained that a couple of months previously she had been raped by a stranger in a secluded spot half-way between her home and that of her then boyfriend.

In interview, with her mother present, the girl says that she had left her boyfriend's house to return home and took a short cut around the rear of a group of bungalows reserved for pensioners. As she did so, she was grabbed from behind by a man who dragged her about 50 metres to a fence. He undid her jeans and pushed them down towards her knees. He forced her legs apart and raped her. He then ran off.

She walked home, ran upstairs, removed her clothing and placed it in the laundry. She ran a bath and lay in it, feeling violated. She was not sexually experienced.

After the girl had had a termination, the police interviewed her again, this time alone. In this interview the girl admitted that she was sexually active and had had unprotected intercourse earlier that evening with her boyfriend. The police recovered her jeans and suggested that it would have been physically difficult for the rapist to have penetrated her with the jeans around her knees.

This is a busy squad with a heavy workload and not every complaint of sexual assault can be fully investigated. If you were the officer-in-charge would you decide to continue this investigation or not?

Which of the following continuing investigations would you cease investigating in order to divert staff to the one described above?

- Investigation of an internet child pornography ring.
- Illegal importation of women migrants from developing countries for the sex trade.
- Gang rape of an elderly woman.
- Grooming of a three-year-old by a man with convictions for paedophile offences.

In groups, discuss your answer. Bear in mind that if you decide to pursue this investigation there will be others that will not be investigated. It is your responsibility to allocate staff so as to achieve the greatest likelihood of prosecution and conviction.

Comment

While this investigation was continuing, across the city in another division a well-known sexual offender had been arrested for attempted rape. Under interrogation he freely admitted to the offence in question and began to admit to a string of other offences. Not all of these offences were listed on the computer, but by chance a detective dealing with this case happened to mention to a colleague dealing with the 14-year-old girl the circumstances of the rape that couldn't be connected to anything on the database. The location and date of the rape to which the man was admitting fitted the details of the 14-year-old girl's case. DNA from the aborted foetus confirmed that the man was the biological father. The man was sentenced to 14 years' imprisonment for this and other rapes.

The tide of legislation

Go to the website: **www.opsi.gov.uk/acts**.

- Count how many Acts of Parliament there have been over the previous 12 months.
- How many of them dealt with criminal issues?
- Choose any one of these criminal Acts of Parliament and follow the web link to the text.

PRACTICAL TASK

- *Read down the 'Contents' page and see how many offences you can identify (in most cases this is best done by several of you working together, because the number of offences is often quite large).*

Comment: *learning outcome*

You will appreciate from doing this task just how much legislation pours out of Parliament that the police are expected to enforce.

At the police station, a member of staff will compile a report that will be forwarded to others in the bureaucracy who will decide whether the incident reported actually is a crime or not and, if so, into which criminal category it falls. The bureaucratic process of recording 'offences known to the police' concludes with the police force annually reporting to the Home Office the offences reported within its area that are 'notifiable'. Not all offences are notifiable because the Home Office is not concerned about dogs fouling pavements and the like. This is more than a bureaucratic obligation, because crimes that are notifiable signal to the police that the Home Office considers these offences to be important and serious. It indicates those offences to which the police should pay attention and perhaps try to reduce in number. One way of reducing them might be to interpret the offence so as to avoid recording incidents as notifiable wherever possible. A common saying among police officers is 'What gets measured, gets done.'

This is not the only bureaucratic influence that is felt by the police: during the past decade, the Home Office also imposed upon police forces certain targets designed to steer the behaviour of police officers from a distance. This had an influence on what was recorded, because the most prominent target was the number of offenders brought to justice, which seems to have encouraged police officers unnecessarily to arrest children for minor offences. In order to do this, the offence would need to be recorded – so a playground fight became an assault. Seeing the error of its ways (but not publicly admitting it!) a Home Office Green Paper (2008) promised to abandon such targets. In future, policing will rely upon officers using their common sense. In short, there is a series of steps, each of which involves interpretation of what is a criminal offence and decisions about how to treat it.

Crime surveys

The second source of information about the extent of crime is the annual British Crime Survey conducted by the Home Office. This involves asking a sample of almost 50,000 people whether they have suffered any of a list of incidents in the past year or so. The list contains ordinary language descriptions of criminal offences and those interviewees who reply that they have suffered particular incidents are asked for details. However, this still does not include *all* crimes, because people under 16 years of age are excluded and so too are businesses (although there is a separate occasional survey of commercial premises). Nevertheless, it reveals more than double the number of incidents than are reported to police (what used to be called 'the dark figure of crime' by criminologists until crime surveys began to shine a light on it) – in 2006–07 it amounted to over 11 million.

The most obvious conclusion to draw is that people do not report to the police all the incidents they consider to be crimes. Moreover, they do not report crimes in a consistent manner. The Home Office estimates that the theft of motor vehicles is almost always reported (probably for insurance reasons), whereas only three in ten episodes of vandalism are reported. Furthermore, serious offences such as robbery and wounding are only reported to police on less than half the occasions on which they occur.

Crime *recording* by the police

Added to this, police do not record all the offences that people report to them, for a variety of reasons. The Home Office estimates that, on average, only 70 per cent of incidents reported in the crime survey are recorded by the police as crimes. Again, there are differences in recording rates between offences. Crimes connected with the theft of motor vehicles are recorded at a high rate, whereas only 80 per cent of woundings are recorded (for a wider discussion, see Newburn, 2007). This is called the 'attrition rate', which is the rate at which offenders and their offences disappear from the system. Chambers and Millar (1983) examined how sexual assaults were dealt with under the Scottish criminal justice system and concluded with a chart so complex that it cannot be reproduced here, but the result was that, taking as a baseline of 100 per cent those offences reported to and recorded by the police, only 18 per cent went to court and just 8 per cent resulted in conviction. In England and Wales a Home Office report (Barclay and Tavares, 1999) estimated that, taking British Crime Survey estimates as a baseline of 100 per cent, only about a quarter are recorded officially, and only 2 per cent result in conviction.

What also emerges from criminal statistics is that the vast majority of crime is committed against property rather than people, and is relatively minor. Vandalism is one of the most common crimes to be committed and is very interesting as, despite being a petty offence legally, it looms large in the attitudes of ordinary people about crime. Attitudes to crime are significant because, in recent years, the rate of crime has fallen quite remarkably and on this official statistics and crime surveys agree. Yet, people continue to believe that crime is increasing – what officials at the Home Office describe as the 'reassurance gap'. We will return to this later.

Criminals

Not only are many popular beliefs about crime wrong, but equally misleading is the media-inspired image of criminals. Far from being wily, calculating and malicious, most of those arrested by the police are the flotsam and jetsam of modern societies. Criminals are disproportionately found in particular areas of towns and cities, usually characterised by high levels of deprivation and disorganised lifestyles. Criminals are distinguished by their lack of what social scientists describe as 'social and cultural capital'. In other words, they are pretty isolated and poorly educated. Moreover, they do not travel very far to commit crimes; indeed, a high proportion of those who are victims of crime also have criminal convictions – there is little resemblance to Robin Hood in the criminal population. This is particularly true of violent crime, for those who commit assaults tend overwhelming to be drunken young men, who are just as likely to be those who are assaulted by other drunken young men!

The Darwin Awards

*The Darwin Awards are 'legendary true tales from **www.DarwinAwards.com** commemorating the remains of people who have improved our gene pool by killing themselves in spectacularly stupid ways'.*

Honorable Mention: Dumb Drunk
February 2001, Connecticut, USA

A woman arrested on a drunken driving charge made an odd choice when calling for a ride home. Betty used her one phone call to contact Ken, her drinking companion prior to her arrest, who was visibly drunk when he staggered into police headquarters.

Ken failed a sobriety test. More surprisingly, a routine background check revealed that Betty had recently obtained a legal restraining order against him. A police sergeant explained, 'We cannot allow him to come into contact with her – even if she says it's okay.'

Ken was charged with violating a restraining order and driving while intoxicated. One question remains – was Betty or Ken the more foolish of the pair?

(Source: Darwin Awards 2, p39)

A complaint of indecent exposure

Police received a complaint from a young single mother living in a public housing estate that she had been repeatedly pestered by an adolescent male and he had on several occasions displayed his genitals and made lewd remarks to her. The young woman knew where the offender lived; it was only a few houses away from her own home.

The police visited the young man's home to interview him. Their knock on the door was answered by the boy's mother, who greeted the two officers warmly and invited them in, saying that they were awaiting the arrival of the police – not at all the welcome that the officers had expected!

The officers walked into the sitting room and spoke to the young man, telling him directly of the allegation that had been made against him and inviting a reply, which he did with a flat denial – 'I never done that!' Once the parents heard what the police had come for, their mood changed completely. They dismissed the allegations as ludicrous and told the police to leave. The police said that they were arresting their son on suspicion of 'indecent exposure'. The parents tried to bar the way of the police to the door. The mother was crying and the father visibly angry.

It turned out that the reason for the warm welcome was because their daughter had accused a young man living a few houses away of committing an offence of indecent exposure towards her. It was this indecent exposure that they had imagined the police were investigating.

The popular image of crime is that it is committed by strangers who lurk in dangerous places ready to pounce. Again, the reality is virtually the opposite: all of us are most at danger of serious assault or murder by those closest to us, particularly members of our own family. Rape is overwhelmingly committed by men known to the victim, often someone with whom they have had or are having a sexual relationship. One of the reasons for suspecting the veracity of a complaint of stranger rape by a 14-year-old girl (on page 8) is the infrequency of such occurrences. A great many of those involved in habitual criminality are substance abusers – drunks and drug users – who need to steal so that they can pay for their next drink or drug. Perhaps the most striking feature of criminality is that it is the pastime of young men. Consistently over many years it has been true that, by the time they are 21 years old, roughly a quarter of young men will have acquired a serious criminal conviction and, by the time they reach the age of 30, that proportion will have increased to one third, but thereafter it hardly changes at all. Even 'organised crime' and 'terrorism' don't match up to the lurid imagination of dramatists and novelists; as Joseph Pistone's autobiography of seven years of infiltrating the Mafia in several large US cities teaches us, most of the crime committed was small time.

Donnie Brasco

Donnie Brasco was the pseudonym of FBI agent, Joseph Pistone, whose seven-year undercover penetration of the Mafia in New York City, Chicago and Miami is celebrated in the book and film of the same name. Brasco/Pistone was so successful at infiltrating the Mafia that he was invited to become a 'Wise Guy', the initiation for which entailed killing someone on command. At this point, he was extracted from his undercover role and went into hiding, where he remains, having assumed a new identity, and where he lives in fear of reprisal from the Mafia. His evidence was responsible for the conviction of over two hundred Mafioso and his closest associate within the Mafia, who became his de facto sponsor to become a 'Wise Guy', Sonny Black, was murdered shortly after Donnie Brasco's true identity became known.

Brasco/Pistone paints a portrait of the contemporary Mafia that contradicts many of the media images with which we have become familiar. This is not a world of vastly powerful figures orchestrating major crimes. It is a story of incompetents scraping a living doing minor crimes, such as obtaining cable TV without paying for it. They spend as much time ripping off each other as they do committing crimes against people outside their small circle.

Similar insider stories have emerged from informants within the Provisional IRA during the Troubles in Northern Ireland (McGartland, 1997; Gilmour, 1998). Indeed, it was only because of the ineptitude of the Provos that these informants remained undiscovered for as long as they did!

The important lesson from all this as you aspire to become a police officer is that crime is endemic in towns and cities, especially among male youth living in deprived areas. However, crime is rarely exciting or dangerous; it is overwhelmingly legally petty, more of nuisance value than a serious threat to the lives and well-being of the innocent. Neither does it test the investigative talents of the police officers who deal with it. It is remarkable how often an accused person admits that they have committed an offence, although they may dispute moral culpability as in the oft-heard cry of a violent drunk, 'He deserved it!' If you pause to consider the circumstances in which so many of those who pass through the hands of the police have lived their (often still brief) lives, it evokes pity more than moral outrage.

PRACTICAL TASK

Preventing shoplifting

Shoplifting is among the most prevalent crimes committed. What action could most effectively reduce shoplifting? What role would the police play in preventing shoplifting?

Comment
Shoplifting is facilitated by stores, which use marketing techniques to arouse desire for their products among their customers. They place goods within easy reach and encourage shoppers to touch and hold goods.

Crime-fighting: a heroic vision

The image of policing conveyed by fiction and news media reporting is just as misleading as the impression given about crime and criminality. This image is that the police enforce the law and, by so doing, ensure that the bad guys get their just deserts and the rest of us remain safe in our beds. This depicts the police as the proverbial 'thin blue line' protecting society from lawlessness and it is one to which police officers themselves tenaciously hold, despite their daily experience. No wonder, because it is heroic. In this heroic vision, patrolling officers prevent crime by their presence and the possibility that they will stumble across an offence in progress or use their supposed sixth sense to recognise that something is amiss with a person or situation. Alternatively, once an offence has been committed, the patrol car speeding to the scene of a crime may catch criminals red-handed, probably following a violent struggle. If the criminal escapes, the superior intellectual powers and dogged persistence of detectives will assemble evidence that brings the guilty to justice. The problem of crime in modern societies, from this perspective, is simply that there are not enough police. As an officer quoted in the magazine of the Police Federation of England and Wales would have us believe:

> With more officers the crime rate would tumble in dramatic fashion and the entire community would feel safer. It would ease the biggest fear in the minds of the public which currently is that one day they will become a victim of crime.
>
> *(Police*, May 1997, p6)

PRACTICAL TASK

Television cops

Watch a televised fictional portrayal (not news or documentary) of police and policing (it might be better to record it first). Note carefully how the police are portrayed.

How far does it conform to the following template?

1. A member of the public reports a crime to the police.

2. Detectives examine the scene for 'clues', interview victims and witnesses, and make other inquiries.

3. A suspect is identified and confronted with incontrovertible evidence of his or her 'guilt', resulting in a confession and criminal charges.

(Source: Maguire, 2008)

Comment
Heroic it may be, but true it certainly is not.

Non-arrest is normal procedure

Police officers only infrequently arrest people, even though there may be ample evidence that they have committed offences. The characteristic feature of policing is *under-enforcement of the law*, not its enforcement. It is instructive to note that, when police unions in the USA wish to bring industrial pressure to bear upon the municipalities that employ them, one tactic they employ is the ticket blizzard, when they do rigorously enforce the law and usually succeed in bringing the police organisation and much of local society to a halt!

Chicago night with Pete and Al

Peter and Al were Chicago patrolmen dispatched to a complaint of a 'robbery' in a down-at-heel area adjacent to the business district. They arrived to find the complainant awaiting them on the sidewalk. He explained that he and his partner were having cash-flow problems and had quarrelled over whether to sell a desktop computer in order to raise cash to pay bills. He was alone in the office when his partner's nephews arrived with the intention of taking the computer to sell. He resisted this and the young men beat him up before walking off with the computer. In the glow of the officer's torch it could be seen that his left eye was clearly bruised and he had superficial cuts. He did not know where the nephews could be found, but gave the officers an address where they could find his business partner.

The search for the address led the officers to a surprisingly swanky apartment building. The officers told the concierge their business and the latter phoned the 'business partner'. He refused to see the officers, but told them on the phone that he was not a 'business partner', but had merely loaned the man money to buy a computer. His 'nephews' had repossessed the computer when the man could not pay the loan and had acted in self-defence when they were attacked and the man had pulled a gun on them. He did not know where the nephews were at that moment because they were trying to sell the computer.

The officers returned to the complainant who disputed much of what the other man had said, but he did admit that he had a gun, but had not pulled it on the 'nephews'. They had simply stolen the gun along with the computer. The officers asked for the gun licence and the man admitted that he did not have one – the gun was a war trophy.

(Source: Edited extract from Waddington, 1999)

How many crimes were reported to Pete and Al that Chicago night? What would you expect them to have done about it?

Comment

The dispute over the computer involved a whole array of possible offences, including assault, possession of an unregistered firearm and theft, but the officers concluded that it was better dealt with as a civil dispute between business partners and advised the man with the bruised eye to see a lawyer as soon as possible.

The public demand more than crime-fighting

While a substantial proportion of the public call upon the police for assistance during any one year, only a small minority do so to report crime. Estimates vary according to the precise definitions used, but there is widespread agreement that complaints of crime comprise only a minority of the problems in which the public ask the police to intervene. Research on the work of a typical police control room found that only just over a quarter of calls were reports of suspected crimes and this included a large number of automatic alarms, all of which proved to be activated in error (Waddington, 1993). Perhaps most surprising of all is that victim satisfaction with the police does not seem to rely upon whether the culprit is arrested and prosecuted (Mayhew et al., 1993, 1994). What victims want is to be treated by the police with care and consideration; unfortunately, this is not always what they receive.

CASE STUDY

A complaint of crime

Officers were in the police station being briefed prior to commencing patrol when the telephone in the briefing room rang. An officer answered it and explained to the senior officer that a juvenile had been detained by store detectives in the nearby High Street. The officer responsible for the town centre was dispatched to the store, which he strode through with the confidence of someone who knows exactly where the store detectives and the suspect would be found. He exchanged greetings with the store detectives, with whom he was obviously familiar. They handed to him an already typed statement of evidence. The 14-year-old lad sitting on a seat in the corner of the office staring at the floor was alleged to have removed a sticker that carried a revised price tag of £14 on a pool/snooker cue and left exposed a sticker with the earlier price tag of £13.50.

The youth was taken to the police station, but because of his age he could not be interrogated about the offence except in the presence of an appropriate adult. The youth belonged to a family of travellers and he did not know the numbers of his parents' mobile phones. While the boy knew the way to the campsite, he did not know what it was called or where it was located, so he was taken by the police to find his parents. The campsite was some ten miles away.

On the arrival of the police and the boy, the parents expressed considerable concern at what their son appeared to have done. They eagerly followed the police officer and their son back to the police station. With his parents present, the lad was questioned and readily admitted his offence of trying to obtain the pool/snooker cue by deception, that is, theft. The police officer recommended to his senior officer that the lad be given an instant caution. As soon as the senior officer was free, the lad and his parents were shown into his office; the lad admitted the offence, received a stern warning from the senior officer and was released into the care of his parents. The police officer then completed all the paperwork.

Comment

The whole episode absorbed an entire eight-hour shift. The scale of the theft was fifty pence!

Traditional policing is ill-fitted for crime-fighting

Standard police tactics are notoriously ineffective ways of countering crime. The traditional weapon in the police armoury designed to prevent crime is patrolling. Bayley (1994) estimated that, in 28 separate forces, the proportions of total personnel devoted to patrol work are: 65 per cent in the USA, 64 per cent in Canada, 56 per cent in Britain, 54 per cent in Australia and 40 per cent in Japan. Patrol strength and mode of deployment varies widely among police forces at different times and in different places, but these variations indicate that the number and deployment of officers has little impact on crime rates. Sparsely policed areas fair no worse, and often better, than their more lavishly resourced counterparts, when it comes to preventing and detecting crime. The year-long strike by coal miners led to a significant shift in personnel from the streets of the towns and cities they policed to the coalfields, but there was little discernible impact on crime levels (Waddington, 1985).

The notion that the police catch offenders red-handed at the scene of a crime has little to support it, mainly because, whatever the police do to reduce the time it takes them to respond to a crime complaint, they can do nothing to shrink the much longer delay between the crime occurring and it being brought to their attention (Bieck, 1977). It is now widely accepted that such reactive policing has had little, if any, pay-off in terms of detecting criminals and possibly comes at a considerable cost in police–public relations.

An exhaustive review of research led the Audit Commission (1996) to conclude that traditional styles of patrol are grossly inefficient as a means of crime control. Instead, they recommended intelligence-led policing in which suspects were targeted, evidence was gathered, and then arrests were made. This recommendation had tremendous influence and intelligence-led policing became the dominant refrain of the police during the 1990s and early years of the new millennium, but still the detection rate remained as low as ever, probably because the intelligence-led approach failed to appreciate just how numerous were the persistent repeat offenders responsible for a disproportionate amount of crime and on whom intelligence-led policing was supposed to concentrate. Morgan and Newburn (1997) estimated that this hard core totals at least 300,000 in Britain, enough to swamp police resources several times over.

An exhaustive review of policing methods found that 'One of the most striking observations in our review is the relatively weak evidence there is in support of the standard model of policing' (Weisburd and Eck, 2004, p57). Almost anything is more effective than what the police routinely do, but far more effective than any police intervention is to improve street lighting (Welsh and Farrington, 2008) or mentor juveniles (Tolan et al., 2008).

Detectives rarely detect crime

Media imagery and occasional success in detecting offenders in high-profile cases reinforce the belief that police detect offenders and that this is a deterrent to crime. Detectives can and do hunt down criminals, but this is enormously resource-intensive and could not conceivably be scaled up to deal with the generality of volume crime that is committed.

Greenwood's classic major study of detective work in police forces throughout the USA found that uniformed officers made most arrests and that 'Only about 3 per cent of all . . . arrests [for serious crimes] appeared to result from special investigative efforts where organization, training or skill could make any conceivable difference' (Greenwood, 1980, p36). British detectives also spend much of their time on routine administration rather than anything that could be described as investigation (Tarling and Burrows, 1984). Rather than investigating crime and detecting criminals, detectives actually spend most of their time ensuring that prosecution case files satisfy legal requirements and thus secure convictions. This is not something restricted to British detectives, as Dixon (1997) found the same among Australian officers.

Researchers have found that, unless an eyewitness identifies the perpetrator of a crime very early in any investigation, the chances of conviction almost disappear entirely, and forensic evidence is rarely instrumental in the detection of suspects (Maguire, 2008, p440). Despite advances in investigative resources such as the HOLMES computer system, DNA profiling and CCTV surveillance, very little has changed regarding the amount of crime detected, since that technology is largely used to *confirm* suspicion arrived at by other means, rather than reveal the offender in the way that the television series *CSI* (and its imitators) would have us believe. Yes, the dogged investigation of high-profile crimes does sometimes detect an offender who was not identified at the scene, but this is the very expensive exception to the rule; for the most part, evidence that is not immediately available (such as eyewitnesses who identify the offender) is unlikely to be discovered at all (see Loveday (1995) for a review of this literature).

Differences do exist between police forces in their clear-up rates; however, this seems to owe more to administrative arrangements than to the detection of offenders. In the 1990s there was a minor scandal, when it was discovered that detectives in one force in England were interviewing convicted offenders in prison and encouraging them to admit to as many offences as they could recall, thus inflating the proportion of crimes cleared up compared to other forces.

The view of radical criminologists

Radical criminologists approach the issue of police effectiveness from an entirely different perspective. They draw an invidious comparison between who commits the most damaging crimes and where police resources are concentrated. They point out that criminality found on the streets is pretty low level compared to that perpetrated by corporate executives and other white-collar criminals. One only needs to consider the injury and death caused by unsafe industrial processes and the vast sums misappropriated by various corporate scams to appreciate the seriousness of white-collar crime. Policing, as we normally understand it, concentrates on 'crime on the streets', not 'crime in the suites'. If the police were genuinely a crime-fighting organisation, their priorities would be quite different. However, the criminals who inflict massively more harm than the worst excesses of corporate executives are state officials, who have been responsible for corruption and destruction of the natural environment.

Increases in violence seen during recent years have been linked to the growth of binge drinking, especially in town and city centres in the early hours of the morning as young people leave pubs and clubs. Although it is the young people at whom most criticism is levelled, it was commercial enterprises and local authorities hungry for tax receipts who encouraged the growth of the 24-hour economy and the Labour Government who, on the eve of the 2003 election, sent a text message to a quarter of a million young people reading: 'Cldnt give a XXXX 4 last ordrs? Thn vte Lbr on thrsday 4 extra time' (Hadfield, 2006, p3).

Highway crime

Lawlessness is also endemic on our highways, as motorists (many of whom are respectable and middle class) defy speed restrictions and commit a multitude of actions that amount to violations of the criminal law. Nor are these minor transgressions, as the toll of deaths and injuries, not to mention the cost of damage to property, attest. Yet, traffic policing is regarded by police and public alike as a marginal police responsibility, almost a distraction from real police work. The Home Office apparently agrees and, during the era when police forces chased centrally determined targets, roads policing units were starved of resources and diverted to general policing duties. Speed enforcement was delegated to cameras, but cameras cannot administer breath tests and it seems that driving with excess alcohol increased during this era.

Social scientists also tacitly endorse the view that traffic policing is unimportant, as evidenced by the lack of attention they pay to this aspect of policing. When, in 2003, the Chief Constable of North Wales announced that he would apply the zero-tolerance policy to speed enforcement in his area, there was an immediate scream of outrage in newspapers and on television, until he quietly rescinded the policy! There is an important lesson here for students wishing to join the police: laws are designed to be applied to 'them' not 'us'. 'Them' are imagined to be 'strangers', 'outlaws' and 'bandits'; they are *not* 'ordinary', 'decent', 'respectable' and 'law-abiding' people! (Corbett, 2003).

Just one law enforcer among many

If what we call policing is just a matter of enforcing the law, it would be necessary to include a far wider array of people and agencies in the category 'police'. There is currently a debate raging in academic circles about whether there is anything that distinguishes the police from a host of others who bring to justice wrongdoers (Crawford, 2008). There is certainly a strong case for believing that there are many more law enforcers than we normally consider.

- There are officials responsible for detecting breaches of particular laws, such as immigration, customs and excise, trading standards, tax and television licence evasion, social security fraud, abusive or obscene telephone calls, and much more besides. Social workers may not see law enforcement as their principal responsibility, but when they remove children from families because they are deemed to be 'at risk', this is plainly the enforcement of law.

- There is the army of inspectors who enforce the law on such things as weights and measures, the construction of buildings, health and safety at work, environmental health, pollution and the safety of public transport. Let us not forget that failures in track maintenance killed 31 people at Ladbroke Grove in 1999, four more at Hatfield in 2000 and seven at Potters Bar in 2002, so this is far from being a trivial task.

- Private individuals sometimes acquire enforcement responsibilities by virtue of their employment, such as company auditors who must report any breach of company law to the authorities.

- Security personnel patrol shopping malls and similar locations of mass private property. As agents of the property owner, they have the right to exclude almost anyone who offends not only against the law, but against the finer sensibilities of the clientele the owner wishes to attract to the location (Wakefield, 2003). To these must be added door staff, who provide a rather more robust version of much the same service for devotees of the night-time economy (Hobbs et al., 2003). Behind them is an unseen army of staff who watch CCTV and sometimes direct sworn police officers to those people who they believe are acting suspiciously (Norris et al., 1998). Security guards are also employed to eject protesters from private property and prevent incursions into road-building and other major construction sites (Button, 2003). It is conservatively estimated that, for every sworn police officer, there are two private security operatives – a ratio that seems likely to increase as people find the peace and security they crave within the walls of gated communities.

- To this list should be added others, such as investigative journalists, whose actions have a determining influence on law enforcement agencies. In some cases, journalists expose wrongdoing and then merely hand over their dossiers of evidence to prosecuting authorities in much the same way that the police do.

- Commercial and voluntary organisations, while not mandated to enforce the law, sometimes do so none the less, such as officers of the Royal Society for the Prevention of Cruelty to Animals, Royal Society for the Protection of Birds and National Society for the Prevention of Cruelty to Children. Research for the Royal Commission on Criminal Procedure found that around 20 per cent of all prosecutions were brought by public bodies other than the police (Lidstone et al., 1980), a figure that excludes private individuals and organisations. It is at least arguably the case that many of these organisations are devoted much more exclusively to law enforcement than are the police.

Crime prevention

If we take seriously the notion that it is the *prevention* of crime that defines policing, we need to acknowledge the vast contribution that *non*-police organisations and individuals make to the achievement of this goal. Local authorities that install crime prevention devices in premises on high-crime public housing estates seem to have a considerable impact on rates of residential burglary (Allatt, 1984). Teachers might not see their task as preventing their charges from committing crimes, but undoubtedly truancy and school exclusion play a part in juvenile offending.

Nor can we ignore how 'crime-proof' manufactured goods might or might not be. For instance, British cars were notoriously easy to steal until the 1990s when, under pressure from the government, the industry began to improve the security of motor vehicles until Britain became a world leader in secure vehicles, albeit that it seems to have stimulated alternative ways of stealing cars, such as 'carjacking' and burglary with the intention of stealing car keys and thence the car.

Summary

So what can we conclude from all this?

- Police spend only a minority of their time on crime-fighting.

- Only a tiny proportion of offenders is caught and a smaller proportion still is brought to justice.

- Only a minority of the public requests for police assistance unequivocally involves crime-fighting.

- Police patrol is notoriously ineffective as a purely crime-fighting tactic.

- Detectives spend most of their time on paperwork.

- Policing focuses on small-time crime on the streets rather than the criminality of the suites, or motoring offences, both of which are far more damaging.

- The police are eclipsed by a vast, but unseen, army of other law enforcers and crime preventers.

What influences crime rates?

Criminologists have not produced a single coherent explanation for why crime is committed, by whom and how. What we can be sure of is that crime rates fluctuate noticeably between different countries, different regions (or states) within countries, different towns and cities, and different areas within towns, and even among families. We can also be pretty sure that these fluctuations have little, if anything, to do with the police. If they did, we would expect that, in those places where a particular police policy was operating, it would have a discernible impact on crime rates – distinctly lower if that policy was effective, or higher if it was disastrously ineffective. Yet, crime seems to fluctuate with regard to neither the size, policy and organisation of police forces, nor the laws that the police supposedly enforce, nor the nature of the state that employs them.

New York miracle – fact or fiction?

Much has been made of the so-called 'New York miracle': under Mayor Giuliani and Police Commissioner Bratton, crime levels in New York plummeted following the adoption of zero-tolerance policing. This was celebrated in an essay entitled 'Crime is down in New York City: blame the police' (Bratton, 1997). While this was a tremendous slogan and the reduction in crime ensured that Mayor Giuliani was re-elected, it was not a terribly accurate appraisal, because it did not compare what happened in New York City with what was also happening elsewhere, which was that crime was falling in many cities across North America despite vast differences in policing strategies (Bowling, 1999). Chicago during this period also witnessed significant reductions in crime under a community policing regime. Across the Western world crime has declined despite huge differences in policing styles, structures, policies, legal systems and much else. Criminologists are somewhat embarrassed because they do not have a plausible theory of why crime has declined, but we do know that the usual suspects (which include the police) do not explain it.

Crime and social stability

Over long stretches of time, crime levels have changed – overwhelmingly in an upward direction – despite differences in policing. There was, however, a marked (but little remarked upon) reduction in crime from around the middle of the nineteenth century to the outbreak of the First World War in 1914. The historian Roger Lane (1992) has analysed this period in cities on the east coast of the USA and concludes that what lay behind the reduction was the accumulating disciplines of modern industrial life:

- clocking on for work at set times and working as part of an integrated production process in which everyone relied upon everyone else;

- controls on leisure that saw boisterous games of football removed from the street and located in stadia;

- the growth of state control over the consumption of intoxicants;

- the provision of public services, notably compulsory education, which swept a whole generation of youngsters off the street and into the classroom.

All of this, he concluded, contained waywardness within a strict set of formal and informal social rules.

Lane's thesis receives support from a monumental contemporary study conducted in six US cities by Wesley Skogan (1990), who sought to distinguish neighbourhoods that deteriorated from those that successfully resisted the slide into disorder and decline. He found that the single most important factor that distinguished neighbourhoods was residential stability: if people remained in their neighbourhoods for most, if not all, of their lives, they came to know what was acceptable and felt confident in admonishing others who strayed across the line, because they knew that fellow residents in the neighbourhood shared common standards and would support them. This is an example of what social scientists often call 'social capital' – that is, the extent to which a person is embedded in social networks.

Economy and crime

Further evidence about how crime rates are affected by social currents over which the police have little influence came from a Home Office report (Field, 1999) that reviewed the relationship between the economy and crime throughout the last century. It concluded that:

- in times of economic downturn acquisitive crime increases as some people substitute illicit for legal ways of achieving their material aspirations;

- in times of economic upturn violent crime increases as people can afford to go out, consume alcohol and become involved in fights.

More recently, Wilkinson and Pickett (2008) have assembled a mass of evidence that convincingly demonstrates that, where the gap between those who earn most and those earning least is greatest, the more likely it is that the population of that country will suffer a range of social ills, including crime (Wilkinson, 2008). Compared to the vast social influences that these authors identify, the capacity of 140,000 police officers to have any material effect on crime by preventative patrolling and the threat of detection is puny.

There is an intriguing and vitally important issue buried in this discussion, which is that, for almost the entire twentieth century, crime grew exponentially – that is, at an increasing rate (see Figure 2.2) – and yet politicians did not grow impatient with the police. During Mrs Thatcher's government of the 1980s, expenditure on the police doubled, but so too did crime, while detections almost halved. Despite this apparent legacy of failure, governments have continued to invest in policing. What does this tell us? The answer is that crime-fighting cannot be regarded as the vital task of the police by those who ultimately pay the policing bill. This leaves us with two questions, the answers to which

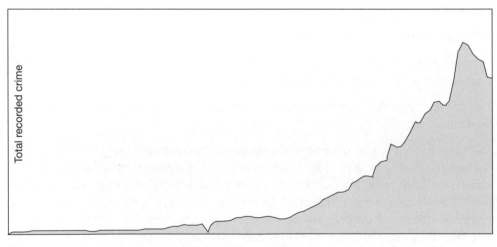

Figure 2.2 Crime in England and Wales, 1898–1999

will dominate much of this book: first, if policing is not mainly devoted to crime-fighting, what is its purpose? Second, why do police officers continue to insist vigorously that their mission is to catch bad guys?

C H A P T E R   S U M M A R Y

The idea that the police are society's bulwark against crime, lawlessness and disorder is simply not credible. If you want a job enforcing the law, there is a host of alternatives to policing that are more likely to satisfy this desire. If you hope to prevent crime, then better be a teacher, or an economist or politician, because that way you will be likely to have a profound effect on the well-being of your fellow citizens.

Police do concern themselves with criminal offences and offenders, but this is not their sole concern. What else do they do? What does it tell us about policing? These are the questions we hope to shed light on in the next chapter.

FURTHER READING

Professor Tim Newburn's *Criminology* (Cullompton: Willan, 2007) is a recently published and comprehensive review of existing criminological knowledge. It is invaluable as an aid to a criminology course. See also Mike Maguire's 'Crime data and statistics' in *The Oxford Handbook of Criminology* (edited by Mike Maguire, Rod Morgan and Robert Reiner, Oxford: Oxford University Press, 2007, pp241–301) for a discussion of the construction of crime statistics.

The importance of crimes committed by individual business people and corporations is discussed by Professor David Nelken in 'White-collar and corporate crime' in the aforementioned *Oxford Handbook of Criminology*, pp733–72.

Brief explanations of 'Clear-up rates', 'Crime', 'Crime prevention', 'Crime reduction', 'Crime statistics' and 'Mentally disordered offenders' can be found in the *Dictionary of Policing* (edited by Tim Newburn and Peter Neyroud, Cullompton: Willan, 2008). Also, for descriptions of 'Crime prevention', 'Crime investigation', 'Victim' and 'Youth', see *The Sage Dictionary of Policing* (edited by Alison Wakefield and Jenny Fleming, London: Sage, 2009).

Tim Newburn has also edited two editions of the *Handbook of Policing* (Cullompton: Willan, 2003 and 2008) and has written a general introduction that is a very useful summary. See also the essay by Mike Maguire on 'Criminal investigation and crime control'.

EFERENCES

Allatt, P (1984) Residential security: containment and displacement of burglary. *Howard Journal*, 23: 99–116.

Audit Commission (1996) *Streetwise: Effective Police Patrol*. London: HMSO.

Barclay, G and Tavares, C (1999) *Information on the Criminal Justice System in England and Wales*. London: Home Office.

Bayley, D H (1994) *Police for the Future*. New York: Oxford University Press.

Bieck, W (1977) *Response Time Analysis*. Kansas City, KS: Kansas City Police Department.

Bowling, B (1999) The rise and fall of New York murder: zero tolerance or crack's decline? *British Journal of Criminology*, 39(4): 531–54.

Bratton, W J (1997) Crime is down in New York City: blame the police, in Dennis, N (ed.) *Zero Tolerance*. London: Institute of Economic Affairs, pp29–43.

Button, M (2003) Private security and the policing of quasi-public space. *International Journal of the Sociology of Law*, 31(3): 227–37.

Chambers, G and Millar, A (1983) *Investigating Sexual Assault*. Edinburgh: HMSO.

Corbett, C (2003) *Car Crime*. Cullompton: Willan.

Crawford, A (2008) Plural policing in the UK: policing beyond the police, in Newburn, T (ed.) *Handbook of Policing*. Cullompton: Willan, pp147–81.

Dixon, D (1997) *Law in Policing: Legal Regulation and Police Practices*. Oxford: Clarendon.

Field, S (1999) *Trends in Crime Revisited*. London: Research, Development and Statistics Directorate, Home Office.

Gilmour, R (1998) *Dead Ground: Infiltrating the IRA*. London: Little Brown.

Greenwood, P W (1980) The Rand study of criminal investigation: the findings and its impact to date, in Clarke, R V G and Hough, J M (eds) *The Effectiveness of Policing*. Aldershot: Gower, pp35–43.

Hadfield, P (2006) *Bar Wars: Contesting the Night in Contemporary British Cities*. Oxford: Oxford University Press.

Hobbs, D, Hadfield, P, Lister, S and Winlow, S (2003) *Bouncers: Violence and Governance in the Night-Time Economy*. Oxford: Oxford University Press.

Home Office (2008) From the neighbourhood to the national: policing our communities together (Green Paper). London: Home Office.

Lane, R (1992) Urban police and crime in nineteenth-century America, in Tonry, M and Morris, N (eds) *Modern Policing*. Chicago, IL: University of Chicago Press, pp1–50.

Lidstone, K W, Hogg, R and Sutcliffe, F (1980) *Prosecutions by Private Individuals and Non-police Agencies*. London: HMSO.

Loveday, B (1995) Crime at the core, in Leishman, F, Loveday, B and Savage, S P (eds) *Core Issues in Policing*. London: Longman, pp73–100.

Maguire, M (2008) Criminal investigation and crime control, in Newburn, T (ed.) *Handbook of Policing*. Cullompton: Willan, pp430–64.

Mayhew, P,Maung, N A and Mirrlees-Black, C (1993) *The 1992 British Crime Survey*. London: HMSO.

Mayhew, P, Mirrlees-Black, C and Maung, N A (1994) *Trends in Crime: Findings from the 1994 British Crime Survey*. London: Home Office Research and Statistics Department.

McGartland, M (1997) *Fifty Dead Men Walking: The Heroic True Story of a British Secret Agent Inside the IRA*. London: Blake.

Morgan, R and Newburn, T (1997) *The Future of Policing*. Oxford: Clarendon.

Newburn, T (2007) *Criminology*. Cullompton: Willan.

Norris, C, Moran, J and Armstrong, G (eds) (1998) *Surveillance, Closed Circuit Television and Social Control*. Aldershot: Ashgate.

President's Commission on Law Enforcement and Administration of Justice (1967) *Task Force Report: 'The Police'*. Washington, DC: US Government Printing Office.

Skogan, W G (1990) *Disorder and Decline*. New York: Free Press.

Surette, R (1998) *Media, Crime and Criminal Justice: Image and Realities.* Belmont, CA: Wadsworth.

Tarling, R and Burrows, J (1984) The work of detectives. *Policing*, 1(1): 57–62.

Tolan, P, Henry, D, Schoeny, M and Bass, A (2008) *Mentoring Interventions to Affect Juvenile Delinquency and Associated Problems*. Oslo: Campbell Collaboration.

Waddington, P A J (1985) Manpower depletion. *Policing* 1(3): 149–60.

Waddington, P A J (1993) *Calling the Police*. Aldershot: Avebury.

Waddington, P A J (1999) *Policing Citizens.* London: UCL Press.

Wakefield, A (2003) *Selling Security: The Private Policing of Public Space*. Cullompton: Willan.

Weisburd, D and Eck, J E (2004) What can police do to reduce crime, disorder, and fear? *The Annals of the American Academy of Political and Social Science*, 593.

Welsh, B C and Farrington, D P (2008) *Effects of Improved Street Lighting on Crime*. Lowell, MA: Campbell Collaboration.

Wilkinson, R (2008) Inequality: the obstacle between us. *Criminal Justice Matters*, 74: 2–3.

Wilkinson, R and Pickett, K (2008) *The Spirit Level: Why More Equal Societies Almost Always Do Better.* London: Allen Lane.

3 What police do

CHAPTER OBJECTIVES

By the end of this chapter you should be able to:

- recognise the enormous breadth of the police role;
- appreciate the extent to which police serve the public;
- embrace the opportunities that this affords for varied, exciting, demanding, challenging and worthwhile work.

Introduction

What this chapter will do is not proceed from some fanciful idea of the cop as crime-fighter, but instead it will:

- ask 'What do the police actually do?';

- highlight the diversity of the policing role.

This chapter challenges you to consider the police and policing in an entirely different way from that popularly portrayed.

What do the police do?

This is a question that has long perplexed scholars who study policing, and still continues to do so. Research conducted in many jurisdictions repeatedly demonstrates that members of the public call upon the police to deal with an enormously wide spectrum of tasks: crime; trouble and disorder; help with emergencies; running messages; and simply to report matters of concern.

Crime

We established in Chapter 2 that policing is not *defined* by crime-related work. Nevertheless, dealing with crime is one part of what the police routinely do: members of the public report crimes to the police that are recorded and responded to, and sometimes suspects are arrested and charged. Much of this work is administrative and bureaucratic. Many police forces employ methods of screening reports of crime made by the public, instead of responding to all of them with the same urgency. A variety of factors determine how the police respond to reports of offences.

A burglary committed while a householder was absent is unlikely to be detected by the immediate attendance of the police, because in all probability the burglars are long gone. Instead, a crime report may be taken over the telephone so that insurance company requirements are satisfied. Also, the occurrence of the offence can be fed into intelligence systems and collated with others so that any pattern leads to an intelligence-led police intervention.

If the report is of a more serious crime, it may be referred to a team of neighbourhood officers who are increasingly supplemented by Police Community Support Officers (PCSOs). Either the neighbourhood officer or one of the PCSOs would attend the scene, speak to those involved and possibly complete crime reports.

Policy Community Support Officers (PCSOs)

PCSOs are civilian, 'unwarranted' police employees with limited powers of detention, whose role it is to keep in touch with local communities in which they patrol in uniform, assisting and advising the people they meet, noting suspicious behaviour and reporting it to the police and, if necessary, intervening in incidents that come to their attention. They increasingly work under the supervision of a neighbourhood police officer who has overall responsibility for local policing in the area, from which the PCSO should not normally be diverted to do other tasks (known as 'abstraction' in policing circles).

If a suspected crime is in progress or continuing, or is likely to lead to more general disorder, a more immediate response by uniformed officers in a car or van or on a motorcycle might be appropriate. The priority given to this response and the speed with which the police would travel to the scene would vary according to the seriousness of the reported crime and the prospects of apprehending an offender. For example, a person who is found dead may have been the victim of murder, but if the death occurred some time before the report was received, little is likely to be gained by rushing to the scene. On the other hand, if the death had occurred in the context of disorder, such as a gang fight, it might be essential for the police to rush to the scene.

The urgency of police response to a reported incident does not depend entirely on its legal seriousness or triviality. If the victim is vulnerable it might justify a swifter response. An otherwise trivial offence occurring to a single, vulnerable person who is or might be emotionally unable to cope with the incident might justify immediate attendance, perhaps supplemented by referral to the neighbourhood officers for follow-up. The offence might be minor criminal damage, but if it is part of a continuing campaign of harassment, it might call for a more serious response.

29

Equally, the characteristics of the offender might cause the response to vary. Riding motorcycles off-road on wasteland may not be the most legally serious offence, but if the riders are young children it may be imperative to intervene speedily before they harm themselves, or pose a danger to others because of their inexperience in riding motorcycles.

So, how the police respond to a report of a crime does not depend wholly upon the degree of criminality involved. Instead, it relies upon an assessment of the context in which the alleged crime has been committed. A straightforward report of crime, such as a burglary discovered some time after it had taken place, is most likely to lead to a report being compiled and no further action, whereas a legally trivial offence might unleash a rapid 'blues and twos' police response.

However, *professional* police officers should not rely on how things are done; instead, they should consider what else could be done. Should information be supplied to local intelligence officers to help detect patterns of activity? Are there other police assets (e.g. crime prevention, child protection) that might be alerted? Might other agencies/partners in local government and the private sector be able to assist?

Trouble and disorder

Already we have strayed into the grey area in which criminal offences blur into diffuse issues of trouble and disorder and in which offences that might have been committed are legally trivial and forbiddingly difficult to investigate.

Consider, for example, a man on board a bus or train who is behaving obnoxiously – shouting obscenities and threats. Insofar as offences are being committed, they will not be serious and, if the man was arrested, a likely outcome would be for 'no further action' (NFA), following him being charged at the police station. Actually, what the bus driver and passengers probably want is simply the removal of this obnoxious individual. If the driver asks for assistance, a police vehicle is likely to be dispatched fairly quickly to rendezvous with the bus. The officers would probably board the bus and ask the driver and passengers what the problem is. Satisfied that there was a problem, the police would invite the man to leave the bus and continue his journey on foot. Usually, that would be the extent of the incident, but what if the man resisted? Well, the likely next step is for the police officers to encourage him by taking hold of each arm, lifting him from his seat and ushering him towards the door of the bus. Suppose he resists more vigorously, stiffening his body and refusing to progress towards the door? Well, now the officers are likely to warn (even threaten) him with arrest if he fails to comply. Ignoring such warnings and threats would inevitably lead to more vigorous action by the officers, who might pull and push the man off the bus. If the man continued to cause a nuisance once on the pavement, he would now be very likely to be arrested for a public order offence, or drunkenness, or found to be in possession of contraband, such as drugs.

Dealing with incidents like this is the 'meat and drink' of daily policing, not only in Britain but throughout the developed world and much of the developing world. However, they should not be ignored because many police officers in all these jurisdictions are likely to dismiss them as 'rubbish' or some such derogatory term. Why do such incidents merit serious attention?

- We must recognise that, however rarely they occur (and thankfully they are very rare), such incidents can sow the seeds of very serious results. On 29 July 2005, Richard Whelan was stabbed seven times (once through the heart) and died of his injuries after remonstrating with Anthony Peart, who had been throwing potato chips at him and his girlfriend on a number 43 bus in north London.

- These types of incidents figure quite highly in complaints being made against police officers, which may be because they do not fit neatly into criminal offences that clearly merit arrest. Instead, officers make recourse to warnings and threats of arrest, and grapple with people in confined spaces, such as on buses.

- This kind of incivility weighs heavily upon feelings of safety and security among the public. Such incivilities are far more numerous and, therefore, more likely to be witnessed by ordinary people. It arouses the concern that, if someone is so unruly that they feel able to shout obscenities in public, they may be less restrained in committing more serious offences.

- As the case of Richard Whelan demonstrates, this is not a misplaced concern on the part of the public. Indeed, researchers have found that those who commit trivial motoring offences, such as parking illegally in bays reserved for the disabled, are closely associated with the commission of other much more serious offences (Corbett, 2003). Commissioner of the New York Police in the early 1990s and author of zero-tolerance policing, Bill Bratton made his reputation in Boston by vigorously cracking down on ticket-dodging. Many people wanted for serious crimes found themselves netted for this minor offence (Bratton, 1997).

Academic researchers often describe dealing with these incidents as 'order maintenance' and/or 'peacekeeping'. It is probably the most valuable function that the police perform. It has now been given greater prominence by the Home Office's commitment to assess police forces by the levels of public satisfaction that they achieve. Many police forces are adopting a 'citizen focus', implicitly opposed to a 'criminality focus'. Often, all that the public want is for a disturbance to their everyday life to cease and the attendance of the police is all that is needed to secure this. Most everyday problems are solved by the public themselves, but occasionally they are not, and when this happens the public needs the reassurance that they can call the police. It enables the public to lead their lives safely and securely. It should be a source of immense job satisfaction for the police.

Regrettably, too few police officers appreciate the value of this very prominent part of their job. *Professional* police officers, however, should consider the wider implications. Are there policies and practices that cause, contribute to or exacerbate such low-level trouble? Does trouble occur in certain places and at particular times? Does such concentration of trouble indicate that there are conditions in the area that promote it? Disorder often masks a more serious situation that can and should be dealt with, but that also invariably involves the mobilisation of others (either within the police or beyond). However, they cannot be mobilised unless the problem is drawn to their attention by officers dealing with its symptoms.

Responding to crime

Fiona Pilkington was a single parent of two children, one of whom, Francecca ('Frankie'), suffered from learning difficulties. The family also suffered persistent bullying from local young people and, on 33 occasions over a seven-year period, Fiona called the local police. Although officers attended repeatedly, no arrests were made and it seems that each call for assistance was treated separately, instead of being recognised as part of a recurring problem. The local parish council brought their concerns about anti-social behaviour in the area to the attention of the police, but again no effective action was taken.

Eventually, in despair, Fiona drove Frankie to a lay-by near their home, soaked the car in petrol and burned herself and her daughter, along with the family pets, to death.

An inquest jury was severely critical of the lack of effective police response to Fiona's repeated calls for assistance. The circumstances were then the subject of an Independent Police Complaints Commission (IPCC) inquiry, which was continuing at the time of writing.

- *What do you consider would have been a suitable response from the police?*

- *Some reports suggested that Fiona was unwilling to pursue prosecution for fear of retaliation. Could the police have done more to help?*

'Domestics'

A type of incident that typifies policing the grey area between crime and non-criminal misconduct is often described by police officers as the 'domestic', but this type of incident also merits special consideration.

The typical domestic is a violent dispute between couples who live together, whether married or not, heterosexual or homosexual. Police may be summoned by one or other party, or by children, or neighbours who are disturbed by the noise. Upon arrival, police usually quell the quarrel, separate the disputing parties, obtain from each of them an account of what caused the disturbance, and possibly arrest one of the couple or broker some informal resolution. Police officers the world over despise domestics, because they find themselves embroiled in tangled webs of allegation and counter-allegation, in which issues of propriety and morality mingle with legal infractions. Frequently, offences will have been committed – criminal damage or minor physical assault are common – but often these are not the prime concern of the disputants. If one party is arrested, the other may refuse to give evidence upon which to prosecute; sometimes the other party will try to intervene to prevent the arrest of their loved one, and they might also make a formal complaint against the arresting officer.

Until 30 years ago, police preferred to deal with such domestics by informal means, but cogent lobbying by feminist campaigners has transformed the domestic. Many police forces now adopt policies that instruct officers to arrest one or both of the offending parties. The reason for this transformation has been the realisation that domestic/ spousal/family violence is likely to be a harbinger of worse things to come. Most murders are committed among people who are already related, and a significant number of those occur between couples living together. Added to this is the misery of many who live in the unremitting shadow of violence, especially women.

American research appeared to show that arresting one of the parties, usually men, reduces the likelihood of future violence, but it has since been realised that the influence of arrest very much depends upon the frequency with which the man has been arrested before. Men with a history of previous arrests are less deterred than those men with a relatively unsullied background (Sherman et al., 1992). Whether a deterrent or not, arresting one or more disputants quells the dispute, at least for a time, and brings violent people to the attention of the criminal justice system.

Beyond the immediate disputants, police officers should also be considering the fate of children and other vulnerable people. If a household is wracked with violent quarrelling, what does that imply about the safety and well-being of any children who are present? Perhaps social workers should be invited to pay attention to such a family.

However, family domestics do not exhaust all the forms of domestic violence that might erupt. Similar conflicts arise between neighbours who quarrel and sometimes resort to violence regarding boundaries of their properties; children's noise, damage arising from miss-hit soccer, tennis and cricket balls; fires lit when laundry is drying; and myriad other causes for complaint. Again, officers responding to the incident are likely to find themselves embroiled in a tangled web of passionately contested facts over matters that to bystanders appear absurdly trivial. Yet, people have died in such circumstances – a pregnant young woman, Krystal Hart, was shot to death on her doorstep in April 2007 over a disputed parking place outside her home.

Sometimes, officers find themselves literally standing between the contending parties, such as the officer who alone faced down a group of armed young men intent on wreaking revenge for harassing phone calls made to one of them by a neighbour to whom he owed money for drugs. As the men advanced across the street, the officer stood in their path and unclipped the holster of his baton. After a few minutes' stand-off, the arrival of other police officers prompted the retreat of the threatening group. (For further details, see Waddington et al., 2006, pp57–8.) As in so many cases, no arrests were made and no offences were reported.

Disputes between landlords and tenants also frequently come to the attention of police officers. Again, it is challenging to unravel guilt and innocence in such tangled relationships. For instance, a landlord phoned the police to complain of paint having been poured over his car by a tenant with whom he was in dispute; upon investigation officers discovered that this offence (which was not denied) was in retaliation for a severe assault by the landlord on the tenant's pregnant girlfriend, who had been violently kicked in the stomach. While the tenant was prosecuted and fined for criminal damage, it was the landlord who was sent to jail for the violent assault. (For further details, see Waddington, 1993, pp89–93.)

So passionate do people become in these circumstances that they act utterly irrationally (see case study).

Destruction of a flat

Four officers in two cars responded to a violent domestic at around 9 p.m. When they arrived, the female occupant of a first-floor flat in a large Victorian house explained that her male partner had become enraged as a result of a quarrel with the landlord and had completely wrecked the flat in which they lived. When the officers looked into the stairwell leading to the flat all they could see was a pile of central-heating radiators, white goods (cooker, refrigerator and the like), and sundry other items. From the first floor the officers could hear the voice of a man crying for help, apparently because he had hurt his ankle and was now unable to move. Because of her relatively diminutive stature, a female officer agreed to climb through the pile of precariously perched household items and attend to the man. She was somewhat apprehensive about the possibility that the pile might collapse, trapping her, but also because, according to the woman, her partner had a visceral dislike of the police.

At the top of the stairs she saw, by the light of a small torch that she was using, the man lying on his back along the landing. Resting on his elbows he repeatedly cried, 'My fucking ankle's broken!' Although he was physically a big man, he looked pathetic and the officer no longer felt afraid. However, he remained volatile – periodically erupting into vituperation against the landlord, interrupted by demands for medical attention – and he was clearly very drunk. Although she now considered him harmless, the officer avoided saying anything that might spark antagonism, such as asking why he had caused such damage.

Looking around, she began to appreciate the scale of the destruction: the landing banister had been completely smashed, leaving a line of spikes of wood pointing upwards. A tyre iron that the man had evidently used as his instrument of destruction lay beside him, so she tossed it aside with the casual remark, 'You won't be needing this, will you?' She checked the man's injuries and saw that, apart from the ankle, they were slight.

By now she had been joined by one of the male officers from the other patrol car that had attended the call and together they began exploring the devastation. She explained that the two officers did not want any 'nasty surprises', such as unappreciated further danger or a dead body in the utterly darkened apartment. As they explored, the officer called down to colleagues below, reassuring them. As they passed where the man lay, she took time to inquire how he was and to reassure him, for she was worried at the obvious ferocity of the destruction.

However, upon return to the landing where the man had lain, the officer found to her horror that the man was no longer there. The smell of burning led her into a bedroom adjacent to the landing. The room was lit by a small table lamp and by its light she could see the man lying in front of an open coal fire pulling hot coals on to the carpet, which was beginning to smoulder. She shouted to her colleague to join her. Together they pulled the man away and began stamping on the flames. She radioed for the Fire Service to attend immediately, but her colleague had now managed to extinguish the flames.

Eventually the Fire Service did arrive and helped to remove the man, who was taken to hospital.

Dealing with domestics in all their variety is a challenging task for police officers – one that they routinely accomplish with remarkable poise, particularly since it is usually young, inexperienced patrol officers who are called upon to do this task. In doing it they bring safety and security into the lives of many who live in the shadow of violence and aggression. The police are beginning to appreciate the significance of this kind of work, but even so it still lacks the status it truly deserves.

There has now accumulated a lengthy catalogue of children abused and murdered under the noses of police officers and social and health workers. Frequently, the problem is that the agencies do not speak to each other, even when police have specialist squads responsible for child protection. Surely, children (sometimes infants) who are starved, beaten, submerged in freezing baths of water, or imprisoned in their homes with abusive parents, all deserve the protection of the police, but repeatedly they have not received it. This amounts to an endemic lack of professionalism on the part of officers responding to repeated calls to deal with domestics involving these families.

The police cannot address all the multiple problems that some families exhibit; just as a paramedic attending a serious road traffic accident cannot do more for a seriously injured casualty than stabilise their condition, a police officer attending a domestic can only bring temporary order and respite. However, the paramedic does not leave the casualty in the road; instead, the casualty is taken to hospital, accompanied by the paramedic, and handed over to the medical staff with an explanation of the injuries and how they were caused. It is the failure of police officers to take ownership of routine domestic incidents, to remain in attendance and to hand them over to other agencies better able to address the long-term issues that lies at the heart of many tragedies. Professional policing demands not only that domestics and other recurrent issues receive more attention, but also that the police accept responsibility for ensuring that other agencies treat them equally seriously. Otherwise, the tragedies of the past will continue to be repeated.

Help with emergencies

The public also turns to the police for help and assistance in dealing with an immensely broad and indefinite array of calamities, for example:

- rescuing people from the effects of disastrous weather and other natural events;

- aeroplane, train and other mass casualty incidents, as well as more routine fires and vehicle collisions;

- helping people locked in or out of premises, or gaining access to people in distress;

- searching for missing vulnerable people, such as young children, and recovering the dead from rivers, shorelines and open country;

- capturing or killing escaped farm or wild animals; and much more besides.

'Help and assistance' ranges from the mundane and personal to the dramatic and society-wide. A good deal of it is routine, such as diverting traffic from road hazards caused by spillages of chemicals, frozen surfaces and so on. It might entail shutting down whole areas if there is danger of an explosion or some comparable calamity, or because of an outbreak of disease, as has happened during successive foot and mouth epidemics. Occasionally, it involves helping people in the gravest danger, such as those in need of food, warmth and possibly medicines that cannot be delivered because of inclement weather. Often police are obliged to depend upon carefully placed signs announcing the closure of a road to motor traffic, or blue and white tape strung across access points – and remarkably few people even think of breaching these barriers, however inconvenient they find them.

One special group whom the police are frequently called upon to help is the mentally ill. This, too, is a challenging task for it may expose the officer to aberrant, bizarre and unpredictable behaviour. It calls upon them to distinguish mental illness from the more mundane problems of drunkenness and substance abuse. It may require them to use force, while at the same time recognising the vulnerability of the person they are dealing with.

Many years ago, American researchers likened the role of the police to that of a 'philosopher, guide and friend' (Cumming et al., 1965), and Maurice Punch described the British police as the 'secret social service' (Punch, 1979). To a remarkable extent, this remains the case, for in time of adversity people turn to the police for help and also for information. It is an opportunity for police officers to demonstrate to ordinary citizens the value of a civil police service.

REFLECTIVE TASK

Violent or what?

A well-built 38-year-old man of African-Caribbean descent, having consumed a modest amount of alcohol, is knocked unconscious in a fight outside a nightclub in the early hours of the morning. He is taken to hospital, where he is so aggressive and uncooperative that medical staff ask the police to remove the man. Police officers drag him outside, arrest him for breach of the peace and place him in a transport vehicle.

On arrival at the police station he is found slumped in the cage at the rear of the vehicle. He is dragged from the vehicle and into the custody suite, in the course of which his trousers fall around his ankles. He is doubly incontinent. He is left lying on the floor, during which time his handcuffs are removed, but he remains on the floor, motionless and unresponsive, where he is left. After 11 minutes it is realised that the man has stopped breathing, officers commence CPR and an ambulance is called. The man is officially pronounced dead at 7.20 a.m.

Appraise the conduct of the officers in this case.

Comment

These are the bare facts surrounding the death of Mr Christopher Alder. The result was that officers were accused of negligence at the coroner's hearing, which returned a verdict of 'unlawful killing' on the part of the police. They were also subjected to a Police Complaints Authority supervised investigation, leading to the trial of five of them on charges including manslaughter, on which they were acquitted; and a subsequent disciplinary hearing in which the charges of neglect of duty against the officers were dismissed. There was then an appeal regarding the trial. Eight years after the incident, an Independent Police Complaints Commission (IPCC) report concluded that the circumstances of Mr Alder's death suggested the influence of institutional racism (as defined by the inquiry into the murder of Stephen Lawrence, chaired by Sir William Macpherson) (Hardwick, 2006).

Whether or not the officers might have been able to save the life of Mr Alder (on this, medical opinion is uncertain), the officers should have placed him in the recovery position and summoned medical assistance. Instead, they left him to die of postural asphyxiation, while they talked casually among themselves. Whatever else it was, professional policing it was not!

Notifying

A form of help and assistance that is quite telling is the responsibility the police assume for notifying and receiving notification. Again, this covers an enormous range of activities, from simply notifying public authorities about some malfunction, such as a burst water main, to telling families of the death of their loved one. If a person has died unexpectedly as the result of suspected crime – whether that is homicide, a vehicle collision, or some other similar cause – the police will most likely send an officer trained in family liaison to break the news as sensitively as possible and obtain information necessary for any investigation. The family liaison officer will maintain contact with the bereaved for some considerable time after the death, especially during protracted legal procedures.

What is policing?

Policing is an enormously varied role. Essentially, it involves intervening in situations that ordinary people feel are beyond them to resolve. Consider a routine traffic accident where someone is injured: the casualty may be lying in the roadway; there may be vehicles blocking passage and debris scattered across the road; and there will undoubtedly be onlookers and probably a group gathered around the casualty. Upon arrival, the police officer may block the road with the patrol vehicle to prevent further danger. As the officer approaches, those gathered around the scene of the accident and especially around the casualty will stand back and, If they do not (perhaps because they're unaware of the officer's presence), they will be asked to stand aside.

If paramedics are not in attendance already, the officer will make an initial assessment of the injuries to the casualty and will possibly radio for the immediate attendance of an ambulance, or if injuries are obviously slight will ask that the ambulance crew be notified accordingly. The officer may invite willing bystanders to undertake tasks such as re-directing traffic or providing blankets to keep the casualty warm. Pretty soon, paramedics will arrive and the officer's attention will turn to investigating what happened. Bystanders will be asked if they saw the collision and, if so, a brief account will be taken and their names and contact details recorded for later investigation.

Drivers of vehicles may be breath tested to determine whether they have exceeded the permissible level of alcohol in their blood. Personal belongings (such as briefcases and handbags) may need to be secured. Vehicle recovery will be organised and the roadway cleared. The casualty may be followed to the hospital and a statement taken about the collision. If the accident involves fatalities, loved ones will need to be informed. This is just a sketch of what a routine accident involves; there is much more to it, such as reassuring the casualty that they are in good hands and preserving their dignity, calming uninjured people who are involved, keeping mere onlookers away and much, much more.

As this routine example shows, for the ambitious officer, policing allows the unrivalled opportunity to serve the public in their time of need. It offers a career that is:

- *varied*: from one moment to the next, it is impossible to say what tasks police officers will be asked to do;

- *exciting*: it is living on the edge, making fateful decisions, often in conditions of poor information;

- *uncertain*: the people and places in which police intervene are often volatile;

- *challenging*: the circumstances that police officers confront have no 'standard operating procedure';

- *demanding*: a wide range of skills and knowledge is needed to adapt to dynamic situations;

- *worthwhile*: police officers have the opportunity to bring safety, security and, above all, order into the lives of people who are often most in need of it.

C H A P T E R   S U M M A R Y

In addition to the above, and probably most of all, policing is *responsible.* The police are only rarely responsible for the causation of the problem, but when they attend to anything they take charge and thereby assume *responsibility*. For example, responsible police officers would not dream of simply abandoning a medical casualty or lost child because it was not their problem. It *is* their problem until it is handed over to others. However, *what* is the problem they are handing over? Surely, dealing only with the symptoms of a problem is to avoid responsibility? This is an avoidance of responsibility that is endemic in policing, hence avoidable problems continue. This is why so many children have died at the hands of their parents, while police officers have repeatedly attended the home because of legally petty offences and other problems (e.g. noise nuisance). This is not only insufficient, it is *irresponsible* and incompatible with *professional* policing.

Even when underlying problems have been brought to the attention of partner agencies (e.g. social services), responsibility should not be regarded as having been shed. The repeated failure of the police to *retain ownership* of low-level disorder problems has contributed to the deaths of that sad parade of children since Maria Caldwell in the early 1970s. However, it goes much deeper than that: police officers see all manner of problems in the raw. They are in a privileged position to identify underlying issues (and many of them do, in the canteen) that police alone are impotent to resolve. *Professional* policing involves working with other agencies to address those problems, so that they may be ameliorated, if not resolved.

It is an onerous role and how officers discharge those responsibilities will be the focus of the next chapter.

The best descriptions and analyses of the wider police role are to be found among the earliest academic engagements with policing as a serious topic of study. Those early pioneers, most notably Egon Bittner in the USA and Michael Banton in Britain, opened the lid on policing to find something very different from what they had expected. These early observations are usefully gathered together in Part B of *Policing: Key Readings*, edited by Tim Newburn (Cullompton: Willan, 2004). A more official endorsement of the wider conception of the police can be found in Lord Scarman's report on the Brixton disorders (Scarman, 1981), especially his distinction between enforcing the law and maintaining 'tranquillity'. It is generally valuable for us all to be aware of our history and there is none better than Clive Emsley's *The English Police* (Harlow: Longman, 1991).

Bratton, W J (1997) Crime is down in New York City: blame the police, in Dennis, N (ed.) *Zero Tolerance*. London: Institute of Economic Affairs, pp29–43.

Corbett, C (2003) *Car Crime*. Cullompton: Willan.

Cumming, E, Cumming, I and Edel, L (1965) Policeman as philosopher, guide and friend. *Social Problems*, 17: 276–86.

Hardwick, N (2006) *Report, dated 27th February 2006, of the Review into the events leading up to and following the death of Christopher Alder on 1st April 1998* (HC 971-1). London: IPCC/The Stationery Office.

Punch, M (1979) The secret social service, in Holdaway, S (ed.) *The British Police*. London: Edward Arnold.

Sherman, L W, Schmidt, J D, Rogan, D P, Smith, D A, Gartin, P R, Colin, F G, Collins, D J and Bacich, A R (1992) The variable effects of arrest on criminal careers – the Milwaukee domestic violence experiment. *Journal of Criminal Law and Criminology*, 83(1): 137–69.

Waddington, P A J (1993) *Calling the Police*. Aldershot: Avebury.

Waddington, P A J, Badger, D and Bull, R (2006) *The Violent Workplace*. Cullompton: Willan.

4 Authority and discretion

CHAPTER OBJECTIVES

By the end of this chapter you should be able to:

- demonstrate that the role of the police officer is to *exercise authority* in circumstances where social order is threatened or has broken down;
- understand how that role as authority on the streets is performed;
- appreciate the challenges that officers face in the performance of their duties.

Introduction

In the previous chapter we described the diversity of the police role, but what is it that gives it coherence? Why do people turn to the police to settle disputes, find missing children, escort the mentally ill to hospital, rescue survivors from accidents, and for an indefinite array of other tasks? That is the question that this chapter will address.

The police as symbols

The issue that arises from the previous chapter, which drew attention to the indefinite array of duties performed by police, is why do the police, and not other agencies, undertake them? Let us extend the example on which the previous chapter concluded. Suppose that a road traffic collision involves a fatality. Why do the police, and not some other agency, convey the most appalling news to the loved one of the deceased? Indeed, police officers will dissuade anyone else from doing this task, so why do they jealously guard such a task themselves? It most certainly is not because police officers enjoy delivering death messages; on the contrary, most police officers dislike it intensely. It calls upon qualities of sensitivity and tact, and exposes them to raw and sometimes harrowing emotion that might crack the façade of detachment. Traffic officers know well that the sight of them standing at the front door with grave looks on their faces will convey the bad news before they have time to open their mouths. So the police insistence on doing this task themselves is not because it is necessarily the most delicate way in which to convey the message.

What trumps all other considerations is that, when a police officer tells a family that their loved one has died tragically, this carries the force of authority. 'Yes, it is true; there is no mistake; this figure of authority must know what he or she is telling us.' If an acquaintance were to tell the family the bad news, they would be likely to refuse to believe it: 'Surely not, there must be some mistake.' They might take steps to verify the information by calling the hospital and it is uncertain whether they would be put through to the appropriate extension or talk to a member of the hospital staff who knows what has happened. If a police officer conveys the bad news, then it is definitive.

In this, *as in many other circumstances*, it is the fact that it is a *police officer* who does something, rather than *what* they do, that matters most.

Patrolling

This is, of course, true of patrolling, especially on foot. When asked, the public repeatedly demand the reappearance on their streets of officers on foot. Walking around in uniform is certainly not a particularly effective form of crime control. The Audit Commission, having considered all the evidence, concluded that it was largely a waste of money and advocated that police redeploy resources away from foot patrol towards intelligence-led operations (Audit Commission, 1996). A dozen years later, the advice of the Audit Commission was consigned to the rubbish bin of history and policing shifted back in favour of foot patrol. Why? Because, during those dozen years, crime actually fell remarkably (although it is unlikely that this was because of anything the police did or did not do), yet the public steadfastly refused to believe it. It became known as the 'reassurance gap' between falling crime rates, on one hand, and perceptions of increased crime, on the other. The restoration of foot patrols was designed to close that gap, because the visible presence of police officers was thought to reassure the public. In other words, it performed a *symbolic* function that far eclipsed any material difference (such as deterring crime and disorder) that it might make.

Police in many societies, especially developed democracies, have much wider symbolic significance. The police officer is often a national icon: the bobby wearing a helmet is a British symbol and souvenir shops bulge with teddy bears dressed as bobbies, plastic police helmets to adorn the heads of infants, police figurines and much else. The Canadian 'Mountie', dressed in scarlet tunic and black riding breeches, the French gendarme in kepi and cloak, and the New York cop wearing the distinctive six-cornered cap, all occupy similar positions of affection. However, not all police are positive symbols: some police instil fear, even by uttering their name – the Gestapo, the secret police and so on. Indeed, democracy is sometimes placed in opposition to the police state, which symbolises the absence of civil rights and liberties. All of this invites us to consider policing and its relationship with the state.

PRACTICAL TASK

- *What other symbols can you identify?*
- *For what do those symbols stand?*
- *Are they positive or negative?*

State authority and the police

If the police are symbols, what do they symbolise? The answer is that they do what it says on the helmet, and not just on the helmet, but also on the shiny buttons of traditional uniforms and the epaulettes of the uniforms of superintendent ranks, not to mention in the insignia of police forces themselves. Look at the police helmet and see what proudly sits atop the badge – *a crown*.

In Britain, the Crown is the symbol of the state and the monarch is the Head of State. The Prime Minister is the head of government, but governments exist to serve the state, not embody it. In order to have an election, the permission of the monarch is necessary; after the election has been held, it is for the monarch to summon the

leader of the most popular political party and invite him or her to form a government. When Parliament is not sitting, government continues under royal prerogative; that is, action is taken in the name of the Crown.

There is more to the state than political institutions. Crucially, the institutions of justice *serve* the Crown. Places in which law is dispensed are called courts because, in previous times, judges were members of the royal *court* who dispensed justice throughout the land. When a judge enters the courtroom it is customary for all present to stand, if they are able to do so, to acknowledge that the judge is the custodian of sovereign state authority. Decisions of courts are not made in the name of political government and it would be a grave affront if any government sought to meddle in the decisions of the courts. Police officers swear allegiance to the Crown and occupy the office of constable, the powers of which derive not from any political institution, nor by delegation from those who employ him or her, but directly from the Crown, and constables are accountable for the exercise of their powers only to the courts.

What is this elusive thing we call state authority? It is what political scientists refer to as 'sovereign power' – note the use of the word 'sovereign', a synonym for 'monarch'. A power is sovereign when it cannot legitimately be trumped. Power can be wrested from a sovereign, as it was by the parliamentary forces of Oliver Cromwell during the English

Civil War, which raged, on and off, between 1642 and 1651, and which witnessed the execution of a reigning monarch, King Charles I. However, if sovereign power is contested, it entails – as it did in this period – an act of war to do it. Those who overpower the sovereign thereby acquire sovereignty themselves.

There is an important corollary to this: it is that sovereignty ultimately rests upon raw power. That is why the British monarch is Commander-in-Chief of the armed forces and so is the President of the United States. They are the heads (however titular) of the biggest gang on the block, or what the English philosopher, Thomas Hobbes (1588–1679), called a 'Leviathan', whose power is justified by the ability to bring civilised order to an otherwise feuding and embattled population. As the historian, political scientist and pioneering sociologist, Max Weber, put it, the state has a monopoly of legitimate force (Weber et al., 1948).

The custodians of that monopoly over fellow citizens are the police. The reason that the public turns to the police in such a wide range of emergencies – major and minor – is not because they have peculiar skills and knowledge to know how best to deal with the situation, but because they have authority. For instance, during the summer floods of 2006, police officers in Gloucestershire went to the assistance of an elderly couple marooned in an isolated rural house, who urgently needed to be evacuated to safety. The water surrounding them was too deep to wade through and even a fire engine became stuck. So the police officers commandeered a big farm tractor and drove it through the deep water to evacuate the couple. In this instance, the police officers asked the farmer's permission to use his tractor, which he freely gave, but had it become necessary there is no doubt that they would have simply taken the tractor. They might even have done so by force.

As the embodiment of the authority of the state, it is to the police officer that people turn when situations have gone awry. Hence, a lone, perhaps young and inexperienced, person occupying the office of constable will be expected to deal with situations with which their fellow citizens cannot. This does not mean rushing in and issuing commands; it means pausing to acquire useful information (e.g. 'Does anyone know who this person is?'); enquiring what resources are available (e.g. 'Is anyone here medically trained?); or consulting local people (e.g. 'Why would anyone do this?'). In times of turmoil and high emotion, slowing the pace of events itself can help resolve problems.

The reason why police patrolling neighbourhoods on foot is thought to reassure the public is because the officer represents the visible presence of sovereign state authority. The local patrolling officer, however benign his or her appearance, is equipped with legal powers to compel compliance (such as 'obstructing a police officer acting in the course of their duty') and the weaponry with which to enforce it. The police are a 'force' and they enforce the law. Police officers on routine patrol carry about their person weapons that are prohibited to fellow citizens. They might ask politely for compliance from those they suspect of wrongdoing, but if that request is spurned, their purpose will be achieved by using as much force as is reasonable and proportionate to the task in hand. If necessary, officers will grapple with those who resist, handcuff them to prevent further or renewed resistance, strike them with their batons, spray CS irritant into their faces, convulse them with an electro-stun weapon (such as the Taser) and, if all else fails and resistance is life-threatening, shoot them and very likely kill them.

As individuals, officers are as frail as any other human being, but if they are unable to prevail they have the means and institutional capacity to assemble such force as will prevail. Behind the vulnerable police officer, there stand squads of riot police and armed police who will subdue resistance by force. If they prove insufficient there is the military, which can be called upon to serve in 'support of the civil power'.

The sequence of police–public encounters

Many years ago, the American researchers Richard Sykes and Edward Brent observed thousands of interactions of all kinds between police and the public. They carefully noted down the exact sequence of behaviour during the encounter. Certain patterns emerged very clearly.

- *The vast majority of exchanges were initiated by the police; that is, police officers acted and members of public reacted.*

- *Typically, this involved the police officers asking questions and members of the public giving answers.*

- *The vast majority of encounters were consensual; that is, people rarely deviated from this reactive position.*

- *Most arrests were conducted without resistance.*

- *Any departure from the standard pattern was likely to lead to arrest. For example, answering a question with a question was a recipe for finding oneself in the back of a police 'cruiser'.*

What does this tell us? Police officers do not enter a situation like others might. They intervene and do so authoritatively and assertively and dominate the subsequent encounter.

(Source: Sykes and Brent, 1983)

PRACTICAL TASK

- *What other symbols of state sovereignty can you identify?*

- *How many of them are related to policing or criminal justice?*

Set apart

The moment that a police officer is sworn into that office, or even when a person declares an ambition to join the police, or attends a vocational degree course leading to a policing career, they invariably find themselves set apart from others. Many will regard them with curiosity, be wary of them, even shun them. Why? Because policing requires that officers perform as a matter of duty tasks that would otherwise be *exceptional*, *exceptionable* or downright *illegal*.

Exceptional

You might consider that walking along a street is wholly unexceptional; it is what millions of people do at some time every day of the week, but they do not walk like the police do. Harking back to an earlier era, Los Angeles cop-turned-novelist Joseph Wambaugh describes how veteran officer 'Bumper' Morgan walked his beat.

> *It was still morning now and I was pretty happy, twirling my stick as I strolled along. I guess I swaggered along. Most beat officers swagger. People expect you to. It shows the hang-toughs you're not afraid, and people expect it. Although they expect an older cop to cock his hat a little so I do that too . . . I started a fancy stick spin . . . I let the baton go bouncing off the sidewalk back into my hand. Three shoeshine kids were watching me, two Mexican, one Negro. The baton trick impressed the hell out of them. I strung it out like a Yo-Yo, did some back twirls and dropped it back into the ring in one smooth motion . . . These little kids probably never saw a beat officer twirled stick before.*
>
> (Wambaugh, 1973, pp25–6)

What Wambaugh understood was that, for a patrolling officer, the street is a stage on which the police officer must perform. Few do so with the panache Bumper Morgan displayed, but there is no alternative to performing because a police officer is a *public* not a private figure. Whether walking, driving or riding, many people will pay attention to the police officer and vehicle if there is one. Unfortunately, many contemporary police officers fail to understand this most basic reality of *being* an officer. The persona they often display is one of fear and anxiety, trying apparently to be inconspicuous; if patrolling in pairs, they engross themselves in conversation with each other, seemingly hoping that no one will intrude into their privacy, or trying to give an impression of being tough guys, perhaps in the hope that intrusive inquiries about the way to this or that location will be deterred.

All this is in stark contrast to the successful patrol officer who understands at the core of his or her being that they are an actor, performing on a stage, and the performance they give should be one of comforting reassurance. Bumper Morgan smiled and joked with people he encountered on the street, particularly kids, drunks and the homeless. He owned the street; it was where he was comfortable. When he saw a couple of guys behaving furtively, perhaps doing a drug deal, he made his presence abundantly clear.

Bumper Morgan is a fictional character – an American version of *Dixon of Dock Green* – but Wambaugh captures a truth, which is that police treat public space as their own private space and they do so because it is! What happens in public space is the business of the police. Professor Randall Collins does not write fiction. His monumental study of violence in all its forms (Collins, 2008) provides a vitally important lesson for all police to learn. When asked what is the best way to avoid becoming a victim of violence, he says it is not to appear as a victim. The police officer who looks comfortable in uniform, is outward facing, smiles at and greets people he or she has never previously met, and hails those who are familiar is also wrapping themselves in a defensive shield.

Big Dave and the skinheads

PC 'Big Dave' had been a PC for 15 years and now was responsible for the town centre in which there stood a public house that catered for young skinheads. Because there had been a history of disorder at this pub the authorities had withdrawn its licence, and on the night in question the pub was celebrating its closure.

The police received intelligence that skinheads from a neighbouring town intended to gatecrash the celebration and cause disorder and violence. Hence, Dave was patrolling the town centre in a personnel carrier accompanied by six PCs. Unfortunately, owing to a major operation in a city 30 miles away, the only PCs available to support Dave were probationers straight out of the training school!

The personnel carrier circled the town centre, passing the pub frequently. As it did so for the umpteenth time, it was evident that a large crowd had gathered in the narrow side street at the corner of which stood the pub. This crowd was angry and the sound of shouted obscenities filled the evening air. Suddenly, a young man reeled out of the crowd directly in front of the now stationary personnel carrier, blood erupting from a wound to his left ear. The officers poured from the carrier and, as the injured man collapsed virtually at their feet, all could see that his ear had almost been ripped from his head.

As Dave hurriedly called for an ambulance, general fighting broke out and the crowd deteriorated into numerous individual fights. The police pulled the combatants apart and pretty soon the fighting subsided into a stand-off between the local skinheads and their neighbours. Between them stood a literal 'thin blue line' of six very young and inexperienced PCs who were understandably nervous.

Wearing a broad smile, Dave wandered slowly into the 'no man's land' between the two contesting groups of skinheads. He ambled across to the local skinheads and picked out a face in the crowd. 'Christ! Are you out already?' he inquired of one skinhead, who looked taken aback by Dave's recognition. 'Couldn't have been "good behaviour"?' Dave joked. 'Yes, it was!', insisted the skinhead, unwittingly confirming that he was indeed the young man Dave had arrested for shoplifting a year or more previously.

Still smiling, Dave ambled over to the neighbouring skinheads, scanning the faces intently. He picked out another youth. 'Didn't I nick ya brother?' he asked. 'Yer, but he's out now and looking for you, ya big prick!' Another confirmation.

So it continued for the half an hour it took for the 'cavalry' to arrive from the city operation. Dave confided that his purpose in doing this was, first, to calm the young PCs: 'Nothing to worry about, guys! All under control! Look, I'm smiling!' Second, he was sending a message to the skinheads: 'We might "lose it" tonight, but we'll be around in the morning, because we know who you are and where you live. We only need a handful and they'll lead us to the rest of you.'

As cars, vans and personnel carriers began screeching to a halt, Dave was already talking to the control room, telling them where he wanted reinforcements to deploy. His strategy was to form a secure corridor between the pub and the nearby railway station. It didn't seem to matter to Dave that he was a PC issuing instructions to fellow PCs, sergeants and inspectors. This was now 'his' operation and he was maintaining control of it.

Once the corridor was in place, Dave ushered up three police dogs and their handlers that had answered his call for assistance. Turning to the local skinheads, he jovially remarked, 'Unless ya want ya balls ripping off, I'd stand over there, if I was you.' Obligingly, a police dog lurched forward on his leash and the skinheads retreated to where Dave had bidden them to go, shouting obscenities and threats about the vengeance they would wreak when Dave was patrolling the town centre alone.

Dave's attention was elsewhere. He approached the neighbouring skinheads, and told them that a train had been halted at the station and would return them to their home town, but they had better hurry because it was due to leave any minute. Reluctantly, the neighbouring skinheads trudged away in the direction of the railway station with a phalanx of riot-clad officers escorting them and the police dogs barking and snarling at their heels.

The 'thin blue line' of the six original PCs brought up the rear, all of them now a little older and more confident. Dave said how he wanted them all to feel they had won.

At the railway station there was a reception party of more police who ushered the skinheads on to the train and then boarded after them. Breathing a sigh of relief Dave turned, still smiling broadly, and confided 'Thank Christ for that! I was shitting myself!' He then revealed that the train the skinheads were boarding went nowhere near the neighbouring town. He figured it would take them hours to get home, hopefully in time for breakfast!

Of course there is much more that police officers do that is exceptional: they are duty-bound to approach threat and danger from which ordinary citizens are free to retreat. They handle the dead: in a society where tragically many elderly people die alone (or even worse in the sole company of a pet dog or cat), neighbours are unlikely to be alerted until the stench of rotting flesh permeates beyond the confines of the corpse's dwelling. Police officers will find themselves dispatched to gain entry to the dwelling, where they might find the partially devoured remains of the deceased. It is not a world to which most people beyond the police are privy.

Nor are most people privy to the degradation in some people's lives. Vacated buildings in which drugs and alcohol are traded and consumed become vermin-infested hovels where inhabitants have defecated wherever and whenever they felt the need. Few others experience the squalor that is the daily locale for most policing. Neither do they encounter people whose lives are so disorganised and depraved that parents think nothing of their children binge drinking and smoking dope while they have casual sex in the same room. (Believe us, all of these examples are drawn from personal experience of observing police officers performing their duties, one of us as a 30-year veteran and the other as a researcher.)

As a police officer, one is duty-bound to deal with episodes involving people and places into which no one else would ever consider venturing. Police officers frequently offer vivid descriptions of their work that involve close encounters with excrement.

Exceptionable

A police officer who greets perfect strangers as established friends may be acting unusually, but few would take exception to it. However, police often transcend the boundaries of otherwise acceptable conduct. The researcher Jonathan Rubenstein (1973) noted that police officers look at strangers differently from how others do. The normal convention in Western society is that, if eye contact is made with a stranger, it is quickly averted. To do otherwise may appear intrusive, even intimidating or challenging. But it is exactly what the police do, because it affirms their authority to look at anyone in a public place. Of course, it is better done with a pleasant expression that communicates, 'Don't worry, I'm just making sure you're OK!' However, it does not stop at how police deploy their gaze as an instrument of authority; it takes on far more tangible forms. Police officers may stop people and enquire who they are, where they live and what they are doing – insufferable intrusions into liberty if done by someone other than a police officer.

This doesn't stop at the street. In a research study that compared the experience of violence suffered by social workers, mental health professionals and police officers (Waddington et al., 2006), it was found that police officers entered private dwellings in ways quite different from those of social workers and mental health professionals. The latter entered as 'guests': they rang the bell or knocked on the door, waited for a reply and to be invited in, went into whichever room they were directed to and sat where bidden. It was a recipe for vulnerability, as some found to their cost.

Police officers did not behave like that – they entered the homes of others as figures of authority. This is not how a guest behaves; police may be guests who are invited for all manner of purposes, but when the occasion demands, they are not guests but figures of authority who exercise that authority even within the privacy of the home – something that would be quite exceptionable if done by almost anyone else.

CASE STUDY

A complaint of domestic violence

A call had been received at the police control room from a woman alleging that she was the victim of domestic violence. Before the call was concluded the line was disconnected, indicating that a third party had terminated the call – obvious grounds for alarm. A police patrol was urgently dispatched to the address – a flat in a dilapidated block of flats. The two officers went to the door and banged heavily upon it. The door opened only a little and a woman apologised for the inconvenience, but reassured the officers that nothing was amiss, just a misunderstanding between herself and her partner. One of the officers rested his hand on the door and gently pushed it open against the resistance of the woman. As he did so, he explained that he could not rely on her account, because the man who was assaulting her may be behind the door with a knife.

The officers walked into a living room with a kitchen area at the far end. On a divan bed pushed against an outer wall sat a young man next to a child's cot in which lay a small infant. One officer casually strolled to the kitchen area with the intention of blocking access to the knives and other weaponry that probably lay there. His companion began questioning the woman about the incident. Meanwhile, the man on the bed was engrossed in a telephone conversation.

Finishing his questioning of the woman, the officer turned to the man and asked if he would not mind terminating his phone call so that he too might be questioned. The man ignored the officer. So the invitation to terminate the phone call was repeated, this time as an instruction. Again the officer was ignored. So he walked to where the phone was plugged in and pulled the connection from the wall. Turning to the man, he said 'I did ask!'

Illegal

Police officers habitually perform actions that, if done by anyone else, would be *ipso facto* illegal. Let us return to Bumper Morgan walking his beat. Apart from the display of twirling and bouncing his baton, we should note that the prop in this performance is a *weapon* – what would otherwise be called a 'cosh' or 'cudgel'. If anyone else did this they would need a compelling reason for carrying such a weapon. But that is only the beginning: even Britain's unarmed police are festooned with weaponry unavailable legally to others – handcuffs, CS spray and possibly a Taser; some do carry guns that are prohibited to anyone other than themselves and the military.

Police officers also, from time to time, arrest fellow citizens – what would in other circumstances inevitably amount to assault. To gain entry to premises, police sometimes smash down doors. They might be accompanied by large fearsome dogs or ride astride imposing horses. In some circumstances, police may be attired for battle, wearing riot helmets and body armour and carrying shields. Most exceptionally, police use violence (euphemised as 'force') as an instrument of their profession.

Discretion

This is not the full extent of police power, for they routinely employ something far more potent than physical force – *they selectively apply legal sanctions*.

It is often imagined that police officers simply *enforce* the law. 'I saw you go through that red traffic light and must, therefore, caution you that you need not say anything . . ..' The truth is that, if the police even attempted to enforce every criminal statute, normal life would rapidly come to a halt, because there are simply too many laws for them all to be enforced. If we add to this mix the ways in which the courts have interpreted the law, the impossible becomes inconceivable. The eminent professor of criminal law, A T H (Tony) Smith, once demonstrated that a little known provision of the Criminal Justice Act 1969, when taken in combination with judicial interpretation of the word 'intoxication' in wholly unrelated cases, effectively made and continues to make it a criminal offence to be in a public place having imbibed alcohol (Smith, 1982).

So simple neutral enforcement of the law whenever and wherever it is breached is not an option. There are some jurisdictions in which the police maintain the pretence of full enforcement and the doctrine of legality, but even here the reality is that the law must be applied selectively.

It is this selectivity that is known as 'discretion'. It is an apt term, for it does not mean that a police officer (or any other of a host of officials who must selectively apply rules) can choose to enforce whatever law or rule he or she feels is appropriate. To do so would be *officious*. To apply the law selectively and at the same time properly entails exercising discretion, that is, assessing every case on its merits. Even where a serious law has clearly been broken, it may still be inappropriate *in all the circumstances* to arrest someone.

REFLECTIVE TASK

Applying the law with discretion

A middle-aged resident of a house on an estate who has never come to the attention of the police before has pushed over a youth causing grazing to the youth's arm, an incident that on the face of it constitutes a common assault. The circumstances are that the man's wife is dying of a distressing degenerative illness – motor neuron disease – which progressively prevents a person moving any muscle, not even being able to swallow. Married for 30 years, the man has resisted calls for his wife to be taken into hospital to receive palliative care. Instead, he has given up his career as an accountant in a large company to care night and day for his wife. She is now in the final stages of the illness and her husband regularly wakes throughout the night to care for her.

Alongside the house is a footpath that leads on to open ground. Unfortunately, youths in the area have come to regard the footpath as a short cut along which to ride their motorcycles and race each other around the open ground beyond. The man has remonstrated repeatedly with the youths, telling of his wife's condition and appealing for them not to cause disturbance. Not only have some of the youths failed to heed his pleas, they have taken to causing additional distress by throwing pebbles at bedroom windows late at night when the man has been attending to his wife's needs. Lacking sleep and suffering persistent noise and nuisance, the man has been nearing the end of his tether.

On the day in question, a young man was in the roadway immediately outside the man's house quite late at night. He was not among the youths who had caused the man so much distress. Instead, he was visiting his new girlfriend across the street – a nice girl from a respectable family who had supported the man as much as they could during his wife's illness. At the end of the visit the young man's motorcycle failed to start and, when it did, it wasn't running properly. The youth fiddled with the engine, making adjustments, each time kick-starting the engine, which roared and spluttered. The man's wife was awakened from one of her few periods of deep sleep by this cacophony and was startled by the noise, crying uncontrollably. Unable to settle her, the man rushed out of his house, grabbing a walking stick as he went, and attacked the youth on the motorcycle, belabouring him with the walking stick. When the youth's girlfriend tried to intervene, she too was struck a nasty blow to the arm that caused bruising.

The police were called. What action would you think was appropriate?

Comment

In circumstances such as those described here there is clearly a breach of the law. Two innocent people have been attacked and one of them has received a nasty injury. However, if the officer simply arrests the man and takes him to the police station, consider the following.

- *What will happen to the man's wife who needs constant care?*

- *Is it understandable that the man was pushed inadvertently beyond any reasonable limit?*

- *What would this do to quell the cause of the man's anger – the youths causing noise and nuisance?*

- *How will it advantage those living in the community?*

Though an acute example, it is not an unrealistic one. It calls upon the police to be sensitive to all parties to the situation: to the man driven witless by noise and nuisance; to the hapless youth whose motorcycle would not start; to the girlfriend struck on the arm and her parents who have supported the man in the past. This sensitivity should also be extended to the youths who are riding motorcycles along a footpath where they are forbidden. It would be easy to brand them as the villains, but why are they using open ground to entertain themselves by riding their bikes where they are forbidden?

Exercising discretion comes close to the police officer acting as judge, jury and even executioner in some situations. It may call upon him or her to mediate between the parties, perhaps to arrange reparation of some sort from the man to the girlfriend. It may involve putting the man in touch with state and voluntary agencies who may be able to provide greater support for him in caring for his wife. It may entail the police officer taking action against the youths who ride their motorcycles along the path, but also it may require liaison with the local authority to redesign the footpath to discourage its misuse. Compared to exercising discretion properly and thoroughly, law enforcement is simple ('You're nicked!').

Discretion can also be dangerous, because judgement can be a cloak that hides stereo-typing and prejudice. Let us tweak our example just a little. Suppose that the man concerned had a long history of intolerance of others and was becoming agitated long before his wife became ill. Now, one might begin to wonder whether the circumstances revealed more about his threshold of tolerance than it did the intrinsic noise and nuisance caused by motorcycles revving as they drove illegally along the path. Perhaps he mishandled the situation and needlessly antagonised the youths, perversely encouraging them to make a greater nuisance of themselves. These are the complexities one gets into when exercising police discretion. However, suppose now that the man's first language is not English and he sometimes struggles to express himself in this, for him, foreign tongue. Equally, suppose he is a member of an ethnic minority whose experience of life in this country is that of subtle and not-so-subtle racism?

It has been the exercise of discretion that has persistently provoked allegations of police racism. For instance, patrolling officers see youths walking along a dark street where there have been several recent thefts from parked cars. Some of the youths have the hoods of their jackets pulled up even though the evening is dry. The officers suspect that the youths are seeking to avoid identification by CCTV cameras in the area and so stop the youths to ask them what they are doing. The youths respond by accusing the police of always picking on them for no good reason. The officers respond by searching the youths either for implements that might be used to force access to parked cars or for stolen goods, neither of which are found. Were the officers justified in suspecting the youths? There is no offence of walking with a hood over one's head. What justification have the police officers for suspecting that thefts from vehicles are likely to be committed by young people, rather than adults? If the young men also belong to an ethnic minority it is tempting to imagine that it is their ethnicity, rather than their attire, that has prompted the stop and search, especially if those youths are repeatedly stopped and searched without any contraband being found.

If the legal powers that the police enjoy are onerous, discretion in their use can be even more so. It means not only having to arrive at judgements in often complex and unclear circumstances, but to do so not in the quiet atmosphere of the courtroom and after due deliberation, but 'on the hoof', while passions are still aroused and indignation burns white hot. No wonder it has been found that police officers find dealing with straightforward criminal incidents so much easier than sorting out the tangled relationships between people living and working in communities. By the same token, sorting out those problems can add enormously to the quality of life of those who live in the area that is successfully policed with discretion.

It is vitally important that police officers are *reflexively aware* of why they exercise their discretion as they do. In many cases it is prudent for officers to record their reasons for taking the decisions they did. The problem is that policing is suffused with discretion and it is beyond the ability of anyone to be reflexively aware of *every* exercise of discretion and it is always the least obvious decisions that come back to bite one!

CHAPTER SUMMARY

In sum, the police officer is not just a citizen in uniform, but is empowered to act in ways that exceed the boundaries of normal social relationships. This is an awesome responsibility that is granted to the police by fellow citizens. Used properly, police power can be used to enhance the safety and security of fellow citizens, which is why so many of the latter demand to see a police presence in public places. However, if misused it can prove oppressive. It can make life a misery and can amount to the wholesale abuse of human rights, as it has done in many authoritarian regimes. At its worst, it can be the instrument of torture and murder.

Even more powerful is the obligation of a police officer to apply the law with discretion and not simply to react to every infraction by arresting the lawbreakers. Used with care and appropriately, discretion can ensure that only those truly responsible for wrongdoing come to the attention of the criminal justice system. Used carelessly or maliciously, it can damage communities and make the task of policing them much more difficult.

The power that is vested in police officers must be used responsibly and professionally. This entails officers remaining continuously aware of the extraordinary nature of their profession and alert to any departure from the highest standards of conduct. Although the character of 'Gene Hunt' in the BBC TV series *Life on Mars* and *Ashes to Ashes* is wildly overdrawn, it is not a gross misrepresentation of some of the attitudes prevalent in the 1970s, especially in large urban police forces in areas of high ethnic minority settlement, which brought disgrace upon the police and public opprobrium. It undermined the trust that others – most notably the courts – had unswervingly given.

Max Weber (1864–1920), once described those who acted on behalf of the state (as do the police) as 'consorting with diabolical powers' (Weber et al., 1948). He was correct! That is why only the highest standards of professionalism are good enough for the police of a democracy.

REFERENCES

Audit Commission (1996) *Streetwise: Effective Police Patrol*. London: HMSO.

Collins, R (2008) *Violence: A Micro-Sociological Theory*. Princeton, NJ: Princeton University Press.

Rubenstein, J (1973) *City Police*. New York: Farrar, Strauss and Giroux.

Smith, A T H (1982) Breaching the peace and disturbing the public quiet. *Public Law* (Summer): 212–18.

Sykes, R E and Brent, E E (1983) *Policing: A Social Behaviourist Perspective*. New Brunswick, NJ: Rutgers University Press.

Waddington, P A J, Badger, D and Bull, R (2006) *The Violent Workplace*. Cullompton: Willan.

Wambaugh, J (1973) *The Blue Knight*. London: Sphere Books.

Weber, M, Mills, C W and Gerth, H H (1948) *From Max Weber: Essays in Sociology*. London: Kegan Paul.

5   A people business

Introduction

Throughout democratic jurisdictions a controversy has long raged regarding whether it is best to describe the police as a 'force' or a 'service'. The pendulum has swung from one to the other, with the inevitable cost of revised signage and corporate logos. In this book we have avoided using either term and prefer simply to describe the police as 'the police', for the police are neither force nor service, while at the same time being both!

Force or service?

In the previous chapter we emphasised the power that the police have over their fellow citizens. There is just one characteristic that all police everywhere in the world have in common: they will, if pushed hard enough, *kill* their fellow citizens. They vary enormously in the extent to which they need to be pushed before they resort to using lethal force, but all of them share the *capacity* to use it. This is what it means to use sovereign power.

Yet it is a deep paradox of policing (and the state that the police serve) that no police can function by the use of force alone, or even as a commonly employed tactic. That is not to say that some have not tried: authoritarian regimes, such as the Nazis who ruled Germany and occupied Europe during the Second World War; or the Soviet Empire that Stalin built and that successive generations of apparatchiks sustained; or the apartheid state of South Africa, all relied on naked force. However, in all cases state power proved to be brittle and collapsed.

CASE STUDY

The force of apartheid

The apartheid regime in South Africa collapsed in 1994, when Nelson Mandela was released from prison and elected as President in the country's first democratic election. The apartheid state was notorious for its brutality. Its police routinely patrolled the African townships on the periphery of major cities in large armoured vehicles, called 'Caspirs', on which were mounted twin general-purpose machine guns. Officers were equipped with a formidable armoury of weapons: each officer carried a 9 mm self-loading pistol, supplemented by 'battle' shotguns carrying 50 cartridges, assault rifles firing 5.56 mm military ammunition, and Uzi sub-machine guns. They had available rubber bullets, and stun, smoke and tear gas grenades. Yet the townships had become 'ungovernable' by the late 1970s and police officers were killed in large numbers, as were members of the township populations who frequently fought them.

The might of the apartheid state was unable to resist the mass opposition of a largely unarmed African population.

PRACTICAL TASK

Using the internet, explore the success of other oppressive policing systems, for example those of the Soviet states, of the British Empire and in the southern USA before the 1970s, and the policing of the Palestinian Occupied Territories by Israeli police.

As Max Weber pointed out long ago, to rule at the point of a gun is wasteful: it requires that, for everyone who is ruled, there must be someone pointing the gun, and who rules them? Thus, while ultimately the state (and its servants, the police) rely upon might, they cannot afford to do so very often. Instead, the police seek to gain compliance of citizens through the use of *legitimate* power.

Consider the humble routine task of stopping traffic: when police officers step into the road and raise an arm as a signal for traffic to stop they are exercising legitimate power, for they do not have any direct control over the speed of the vehicles approaching them. They rely on the drivers respecting that they have the *right* to demand that they stop, however inconvenient it might be. If a cyclist decided not to stop and to weave their way around the officer and ride off into the distance, there is precious little that the officer could do to prevent it or impose some later penalty. It is commonplace for even those who are committing serious motoring offences (such as driving without insurance or with excess alcohol in their blood) to stop at the presence of an upraised police officer's arm. While it is true that a very small proportion do not do so (sometimes with tragic results), this should not blind us to the overwhelming pattern of compliance.

How, then, is legitimate power exercised? It is power that is granted to the officer *by the citizen over whom that power is exercised*. In other words, when the driver sees an officer step out into the road and lift his hand in a recognised signal to stop, the driver appreciates that the officer is acting in accordance with his or her duties and applies the brake. Why does the driver apply the brake? Because the driver draws upon a deep well of belief about why having a police force is generally a good thing.

So far, so good, but where do these beliefs spring from? Well, much of it would be absorbed from noting how others behave, so that it becomes a habit: 'It's what we do around here.' This would be supplemented by fictional portrayals in children's books (the kindly Mr Plod in Noddy books), television depictions of valiant cops battling the forces of evil and, of course, first-hand experience.

Throughout their history the British police have striven hard to establish, maintain and sometimes restore their legitimacy in the eyes of the British public. From their installation they had no choice but to do so, for the police were not welcome figures on the streets of early Victorian London – they were despised as 'Peel's Bloody Gang' and the 'plague of Blue Locusts'. When Constable Culley was fatally injured during a riot at Coldbath Field in the East End of London in 1833, an inquest jury *composed of property owners* delivered a verdict of justifiable homicide on the grounds that the police were a brutal bunch and pretty much deserved what they received. Paradoxically, it was this event that swung middle-class sentiment behind the infant Metropolitan Police. Since then, the sadly periodic murders of police officers have been occasions for increasing public approval of the police as a whole, because they vividly portray the police as self-sacrificing in defence of wider society – instead of fearing the police, people sympathise with them and recognise their vulnerability.

Indeed, an essential element of the marketing of the British police has been to emphasise their vulnerability. The British police have never routinely carried firearms in peace time, not because they inherited a tradition of unarmed policing, nor because the streets of Victorian England were tranquil. On the contrary, those police forces in existence prior to the creation of the Metropolitan Police in 1829 were invariably armed (Bow Street Runners carried sabres and pistols, the Mounted Patrol carried horse pistols and the River Police were equipped with blunderbusses; even the decrepit watchmen of provincial towns were often armed to the teeth – if they had any!). The lives of almost all those who migrated into the thriving industrial centres were mired in poverty and degradation. Policing in this environment was a tough job and frequently a violent one.

The decision not to arm the Metropolitan Police (which set a precedent for all those that followed) was a deliberate one and designed explicitly to avoid the New Police being seen as a force of oppression. In other words, it was a bid for legitimacy – reassuring the public that they had no reason to fear the police, who were installed as their protectors. It continues today, for example in the logos displayed on police vehicles, such as 'Serving – Protecting – Making the Difference' (West Mercia Police). When the police of formerly authoritarian states emerge into democracy, as in the case of South Africa under apartheid, or periods of violent conflict, as in Northern Ireland, one of the first policy decisions that is taken is to alter the name – from the 'South African Police' and 'Royal Ulster Constabulary', to the 'South African Police *Service*' and 'Police *Service* of Northern Ireland' respectively. The hidden message behind all this marketing is that the police only use their powers to *protect* law-abiding members of the public.

Marketing the police is not solely the province of media consultants and the like; it is something that every police officer does. Watch an episode of any reality TV programme on policing – 'Traffic Cops', 'Cops with Cameras' and so on – and pay attention to how police officers explain themselves during the inserted 'to camera' interviews; they are habitually focused on what the ordinary decent person would want and expect the police to do in the circumstances. Away from the television screen, police officers attending an incident can often be heard appealing to the need to protect the public and satisfy public demands – 'people have complained' an officer might say, even when no one has complained. Much of this is saying to all who would listen: 'I'm not acting here merely on my own behalf, but on behalf of the wider public interest' – vitally important when officers are using discretion.

Community policing

One of the most explicit police marketing campaigns has been the promotion of community policing. Scholars complain that the concept of community policing is so vague as to be meaningless, or, insofar as meaning can be attached to it, is less benign than many imagine. The promised pay-off from community policing has rarely been witnessed; time and again product falls well short of promise. Yet, for 40 years it has been an idea that continues to capture the imagination of politicians, police officials and the public throughout the democratic world. What sustains the resilience of this notion?

Mainly, we contend, it is a response to growing public scepticism towards the police, especially on the part of middle-class intellectuals. In his book *The Culture of Control*, Professor David Garland (2001) argues that, as long as 'volume crime' (theft, burglary, vandalism and the like) remained confined to working-class areas, the comfortable middle classes were prepared to allow delinquency and criminality to be dealt with by social workers, probation officers and other 'welfare' professionals, but, as soon as crime began to lap along the shores of suburbia, it sparked a punitive turn in middle-class opinion. We broadly agree with this, but it is incomplete for what also changed was the visibility of policing.

So long as the working class felt the force of policing, those same middle classes were content to ignore it and rest their faith on the 'thin blue line' keeping the dangerous classes in their place. How the police achieved this was something that those with a delicate disposition felt unnecessary to inquire about too closely. However, when young hooligans began to include among their number dope-smoking middle-class adolescents and university student radicals, policing appeared over the middle-class horizon and it looked none too savoury.

This coincided with a wider socio-political shift, for politics had for a hundred years been organised around the conflict between workers and their employers. This began to change during the 1960s and continued apace thereafter: instead of the colour of a worker's collar being the political dividing line, what came to influence political allegiance rather more was the *type of work* that people did – principally, was it 'person-centred' or not?

On the one hand, there were those occupations that serviced organisations of whatever kind they might be: accountants, engineers, production management and so on, who developed a pretty hard-nosed cast of mind that was attentive to hard facts and the bottom line and, most importantly, treated personnel as a commodity. People working in these occupations tended towards conservativism, especially the neo-liberal variant most closely associated with Mrs Thatcher's government. On the other side of the divide were occupations that served people, notably social welfare and health professionals, educators and others for whom the well-being of people was their concern – these were the bleeding-heart liberals who marched to 'Ban the Bomb' and to 'Save the Whale' (Kriesi, 1989).

Criminal justice had long been a battleground between those with 'hard noses' and those with 'soft hearts', and the legal profession had long harboured those of a liberal persuasion. After all, the abolition of the death penalty for murder fired the starting pistol on the torrent of liberal legislation passed during the 1960s. As politics increasingly realigned and became expressed through single-interest campaign groups – such as *Liberty* (formerly the National Council for Civil Liberties) – so the police found themselves under sustained criticism from sections of the population on which they had previously relied for support.

Initiated by a liberal Chief Constable, John Alderson, and promoted in the wake of inner-city rioting at the beginning of the 1980s by a notably liberal judge, Lord Scarman, community policing amounted to a re-branding of the police to make it more acceptable to liberal opinion. It harked back to a benign image of the policing of bygone days – a mythical Golden Age, when an arrest was achieved by nothing more brutal than a tap on the shoulder accompanied by the instruction 'You'd better come with me, m'lad'! It was a comforting image, but one that repeatedly has come to plague successive generations of police officers, because when something visible happens – for example, the policing of a violent protest or the use of significant force, such as firearms – the invidious contrast between rhetoric and reality is drawn particularly starkly.

Try as they might, few police anywhere in the world have succeeded in sustaining this model of officers entrenched in their communities. The problem is that events intervene and pressing necessity is the 'mother of abstraction' (to misquote a phrase). Officers are 'abstracted' (that is, removed) from community policing duties to deal with all manner of unforeseen contingencies and thus the link between police and residents is broken.

58

Trust

It would be tempting to dismiss community policing as a retreat into sentimentality, but we must be careful not to 'throw the baby out with the bathwater'. Upon closer inspection, we can see dimly through the mythology of community policing that there is more than a grain of truth lurking therein. It is an attempt, however flawed, to address the most fundamental issue in police–public relationships – that of trust.

Suppose a resident in a neighbourhood is suffering a nuisance problem that they have tried to resolve informally, for instance by appealing to those causing the nuisance to desist, and have met little success. In desperation, they may turn to the police and, in response, a patrol officer may arrive to find out what the problem is and possibly intervene. The officer brings to the situation the valuable attributes of independence and neutrality, which enhance trust, but there is also a downside to these attributes: the officer is unlikely to know much about the people involved and the wider context in which the problem has taken place and the officer's engagement with those people will be fleeting. These latter attributes undermine trust, because the officer's understanding of what are often complex circumstances will probably be superficial and therefore any informal or formal resolution is unlikely to be finely tuned to the specifics of the problem.

Moreover, if the officer has no lasting connection with the neighbourhood, there is little likelihood that he or she will inherit the consequences of their own action or inaction. For instance, if their intervention is ineffectual it is unlikely that they *as an individual* will be called back to yet further episodes of nuisance; or, more seriously, if the action is too vigorous and leads, say, to lasting animosity among neighbours, it will not be the individual police officer who gets shunned.

All of this is compounded by the fact that the resident's decision to involve the police is, to a very large extent, irreversible. In effect, the resident has *handed over* the problem to the police and, if the proposed resolution is not to their liking, they cannot simply withdraw saying 'Hang on a minute, this isn't what I had in mind!' Neither is this solely a concern of the public.

CASE STUDY

A plea from a fellow officer

Broadwater Farm estate is notorious as the location in which a police officer was savagely hacked to death during a riot in 1986. By the early 1990s it became almost as prominent as a venue for an illegal drugs market. Dealers openly dealt drugs on an elevated terrace at the heart of the estate and deterred local officers from disturbing them by regular acts of intimidation. The Metropolitan Police response was to mount a huge force (5000+) to storm into the estate, overwhelm resistance, arrest drug dealers and retake the area.

Assembling at the police academy at Hendon, officers were briefed on the operation and their part in it by superiors varying in rank from Assistant Commissioner to Chief Superintendent. However, the last spot on the briefing was reserved for a lowly sergeant, who was responsible for the neighbourhood policing team on the estate. His words were eloquent and profoundly influential. He reminded his audience that whatever they did during the operation would have lasting consequences for him and his team into the indefinite future. He begged them to remain faithful to their professionalism. Of course, he was entitled to expect nothing less.

Police intelligence

Perhaps there is another way: police could finely tune their interventions into the lives of fellow citizens if they were easily able to access the information on which they must rely. One currently fashionable attempt to do that is by cultivating police intelligence, systematised under the rubric of the National Intelligence Model (NIM). The prospectus here is not that of the genial old-time 'copper', but shiny new officers armed with relevant and timely information that enables them clinically to excise problems with surgical precision. Under this manifesto, policing in future will be intelligence-led. According to this prospectus, trust is cultivated by the police acting only against those who deserve their attention.

Evidence against offenders will be forensically accumulated before police swoop, scooping them into the criminal justice system. It is the swing of the pendulum back towards a crime-fighting vision of policing based on an analogy with the Battle of the Atlantic in the Second World War, where intelligence analysts and plotters tried to figure out where the U-boats would attempt to strike next at the convoys ferrying war supplies to the UK from the USA (Grieve, 2009). A contemporary analogy might be an AWACS aircraft scanning the horizon for incoming enemy aircraft and missiles that are proverbial 'needles in haystacks', whose presence needs to be distinguished from the constantly changing background as the AWACS circles above and the enemy aircraft hug the terrain below. It is the backbone of counter-terrorism strategy, which aims to identify incoming jihadists intent on causing mass casualties. It can boast several intercepted bomb plots as evidence that it is effective.

It is certainly a more exciting image of policing than that of 'Mr Plod' of 'Toytown' fame! But it too suffers fundamental problems. The first is the war-fighting analogy on which it is based; for in wartime a known enemy will try to attack predictable targets (such as command and control systems). Yes, they will use camouflage, blending into the background, and so defenders will try to develop means of exposing them, for example by detecting the infra-red radiation emitted by heat sources such as aircraft and missiles. Of course, criminals try to camouflage themselves in much the same way, hiding from pursuing police by skulking in undergrowth and other such places, and the police can detect heat sources too by using helicopters with infra-red cameras that enable ground forces to home in on the fugitive and arrest them, however well concealed they might be to the naked eye.

However, offenders and especially terrorists conceal themselves in a quite different form of camouflage, which is that of the rights afforded to all citizens. One of those rights is that of privacy and this inevitably is compromised by intelligence-led policing, because, in order to distinguish good guys from bad guys, *both* need to be under surveillance. This is the worry expressed by the current British Information Commissioner, Richard Thomas.

Warning! Surveillance Society ahead

Richard Thomas, the Information Commissioner, said:

> *Two years ago I warned that we were in danger of sleepwalking into a surveillance society. Today I fear that we are in fact waking up to a surveillance society that is already all around us. Surveillance activities can be well-intentioned and bring benefits. They may be necessary or desirable – for example to fight terrorism and serious crime, to improve entitlement and access to public and private services, and to improve healthcare. But unseen, uncontrolled or excessive surveillance can foster a climate of suspicion and undermine trust.*
>
> *As ever-more information is collected, shared and used, it intrudes into our private space and leads to decisions which directly influence people's lives. Mistakes can also easily be made with serious consequences – false matches and other cases of mistaken identity, inaccurate facts or inferences, suspicions taken as reality, and breaches of security. I am keen to start a debate about where the lines should be drawn. What is acceptable and what is not?*
>
> *(Source: The Information Commissioner's Office website, www.ico.gov.uk/.)*

Consider the routine surveillance of petrol filling-station forecourts that register on CCTV every vehicle to which petrol is dispensed in order to identify those few who drive off without paying. What is the objection to this? Surely, filling up with petrol is hardly a private act. However, if every petrol station has this surveillance (and most do), it is possible to track journeys made by anyone for any purpose. If such information was valuable, it might be sold. An unfaithful celebrity might be exposed travelling to suspect locations.

Risk

This points us to a further challenge to police legitimacy – intolerance of risk. This emerging tendency has fascinated sociologists because estimates of risk are so often wholly irrational. For instance, people greatly overemphasise the likelihood of criminal victimisation (Allen, 2006), but they also worry about policing itself. For example, there has long been controversy about deaths in custody (IPCC, 2009).

Police, like anyone else, make mistakes; indeed, policing is particularly prone to error because so often police intervene in circumstances that are chaotic, confused, ambiguous and dynamic. Not only are such circumstances likely to result in police failing to provide a service, such as allowing an offender to escape, but equally they may prompt officers into a course of action that results in adverse consequences. The police are not alone in this, for example vaccination against life-threatening disease can also result in long-lasting disability for the few recipients who react adversely to the vaccine.

REFLECTIVE TASK

To pursue or to allow criminals to escape?

Criminologists have known since the mid-1960s that those who commit minor traffic violations tend also to have committed more serious crimes, which means that stopping those people is traffic law enforcement. So, a traffic patrol officer sees a vehicle fail to stop at a traffic light and pursues it. The vehicle refuses to stop when the traffic patrol directs it to and drives off at high speed.

Should the traffic patrol continue to pursue the vehicle when the likelihood is that the driver has imbibed excess alcohol and possibly also drugs, will be uninsured, and is possibly wanted for many offences and therefore desperate to escape?

Comment

If the officer fails to pursue, an offender is likely to escape and the police have fallen short of their duty to apprehend offenders at large (negative error). If the officer decides to pursue the vehicle and the escaping driver loses control, mounts the footpath and collides with passers-by, killing and injuring them, the consequences of chasing a car that has breached a red traffic light and refused to stop for police are grossly disproportionate.

Prevention

The problem of positive error for the police arises from their mandate not only to detect criminals guilty of committing crimes, but also to prevent them from committing those crimes in the first place. Now, there are many ways in which people might be dissuaded from following a path of criminality, but these are almost entirely in the hands of people other than the police – parents, teachers and, most of all, peer groups. What can the police do? Well they can deter criminals by vigilance. What does vigilance entail? It means being aware of who is associating with whom and what they are doing. In other words, it is surveillance, whether the officer is patrolling the streets or viewing a CCTV monitor. Deterrence demands more than passive watching, however – it comes from intervening early to divert those who are intent on committing an offence from achieving their goal. For instance, officers may make it known informally that they are aware of animosities between various gangs and thus, hopefully, forestall open conflict between the gangs.

It also means intervening on the basis of suspicion. This is what police are empowered to do, for example to stop and search those they suspect of being in possession of contraband (such as drugs or stolen property). The level of suspicion required to stop and search someone is well below that necessary to justify arrest. For instance, being in the vicinity of an area known for its drug dealing and acting in a furtive manner may well incline an officer to suspect someone and stop and search them. However, it follows that stop and search will often fail to confirm the suspicions that prompted it. Hence, there is a downside to crime prevention, which is the positive error of invading personal privacy on the basis of mere suspicion (see Case study below).

What we have sought to demonstrate in this section is that, however good police intelligence may be, it is never foolproof and will create positive errors. This can cause resentment, as it has done among several non-white communities throughout Britain in the recent past. Police officers need to appreciate, as often they fail to, that preventative policing tactics, such as stop and search, not only intrude into personal privacy, but also – and more importantly – cast the shadow of suspicion upon those who are stopped and searched in error.

It gets worse: Professor Wesley Skogan examined public attitudes towards the police in six US cities and discovered that encounters that left the public feeling that the police had acted properly had no detectable impact on their approval of the police; whereas encounters that people felt had been badly handled by the police had a profoundly negative effect upon their approval ratings (Skogan, 2006). In other words, good policing is what people expect, but bad policing engenders disapproval or worse – it is a game you can only lose!

CASE STUDY

Drug dogs

Police use drug dogs that are bred for the sensitivity of their noses and specially trained to seek out the smell of prohibited drugs. These dogs are sometimes deployed at locations, such as railway stations, where there is heavy pedestrian traffic that passes through narrow apertures, such as ticket barriers. Often the dogs will detect the smell of drugs already consumed, which does not amount to evidence of current possession. Or someone may have on them the odour of drugs acquired through close physical contact of the kind that is an unpleasant consequence of travelling on congested public transport.

Emotional intelligence

What are the police to do – abstain from tactics (such as stop and search) that expose officers to positive errors and the opprobrium they may bring? No. To abstain from error-prone actions would amount to abandoning any attempt at crime prevention. In a review of 'what works' in policing, the eminent criminologist, Professor Lawrence Sherman, concluded that stop and search was one of few tactics that had an effect (albeit marginal) on crime levels (Sherman et al., 1997). It is also a reasonable inference from research on car crime (Corbett, 2003) that enforcing road traffic legislation not only detects those who violate laws designed to protect road users, but also brings to the attention of the police those who have committed other offences regarded as more serious.

As Larry Sherman is fond of remarking, 'Policing ain't rocket science . . . It's more difficult than that', and it is. Positive errors are as inevitable in policing as they are in medicine, but they need to be managed far more effectively than they are at the moment. It is an aspect of policing that has received little attention, still less analysis, and sensible policies and practice remain to be established. So, what is needed?

First, officers need to appreciate what being stopped and searched actually feels like; perhaps they should experience it for themselves.

PRACTICAL TASK

How do you like it?

Conduct a role-play, to be staged in a public area, in which students play the parts of police officer and suspect in a 'stop and search' encounter.

Comment

This is only a simulation, but few students will avoid feeling embarrassed and probably humiliated. You should never lose sight of just how intrusive routine police procedures can be.

Second, officers need to be aware that it is not *what* they do, but *how* they do it that has the greatest impact on ordinary people's experience of policing. Stop and search has been found to be very closely associated with negative attitudes towards the police. What those stopped and searched complain of is that they are not given an adequate explanation of why they are being stopped and searched, and they feel they are treated disrespectfully.

The implications of this are truly massive and have yet to be fully appreciated by the police at all levels.

Acting justly

Throughout this book we have been at pains to emphasise that the role of the police extends far beyond law enforcement and crime-fighting, and that much of this surplus is of equal, if not greater, value than crime-related police work. However, this should not blind us to the fact that the principal resource that the police have at their disposal is the criminal law. An officer *may* decide to deal with an incident informally or formally, but his or her authority to do so relies on the fact that the formal option exists. So, police authority is firmly rooted in the criminal justice system.

This means far more than simply arresting, charging and prosecuting someone for a criminal offence. It is often forgotten that the criminal justice system does what it says – it dispenses *justice* – and justice is not simply assessed in terms of outcomes. If it was otherwise, there would have been no reason to complain when the Burmese military junta extended the confinement of the pro-democracy activist, Aung San Suu Kyi, on trumped-up charges. It worked, and opposition to their regime was deterred. What fuelled criticism was that Aung San Suu Kyi was convicted *by a process that was unfair and unjust.*

The authority that police officers possess is based on them being 'officers of the *law*', which in democratic systems is law that is fair and just, symbolised by the statue of Justice as a blindfolded woman, holding a set of scales in one hand and a sword in the other, atop the Old Bailey courts in central London. Therefore, in all their dealings with the public it is vitally important that officers sustain and renew the legitimacy of the office of constable by acting fairly and with justice (Tyler, 1990, 2004; Tyler and Huo, 2002). It is not what policing achieves that weighs most heavily on the opinions of those whom officers encounter, but the way in which they conduct themselves. Not the 'what', but the 'how'!

To those who have been victimised, or who feel vulnerable and afraid, the police must be considerate, caring and protective. To those whose faith in the order of routine life may have been gravely disturbed, the police should bring reassurance. To suspects, they must act with conspicuous fairness: listening to what they say in their own defence, weighing the evidence and giving reasons for decisions, and using only as much force as is necessary, however obnoxiously the suspect has behaved or continues to behave. It means cultivating a professional persona in which detachment is combined with compassion.

This is far more easily said than done, although we hasten to add that it is not said nearly as often or as loudly as it should be. It means extending to the most obnoxious people you might encounter (and as a police officer you will encounter obnoxious people aplenty) the same consideration, understanding and fair treatment that you would extend to anyone else in the same circumstances. If this was not difficult enough, contemporary social conditions make it vastly more difficult, for this professional persona cannot be the same for everyone in a multicultural society. To be equally considerate of others means adjusting one's behaviour to the cultural norms of those with whom one is dealing at the time. A confident firm handshake, intended to convey welcome to a stranger, may be far too firm for many non-Western cultures; a reassuring arm around the shoulder of a grieving relative may be considered a gross intrusion.

Police officers often find themselves dealing with situations in which raw emotion is evident. To act professionally in those circumstances relies on emotional intelligence, which is the ability to see oneself as others do. One of the most cataclysmic recent failures of the police – the murder of Stephen Lawrence and its subsequent investigation – did not stem from the failure to convict anyone of this appalling crime. It stemmed, instead, from a repeated failure to appreciate that the grief felt by Mr and Mrs Lawrence mingled with resentment and distrust of the police on the part of many of those who surrounded them. When a new team of officers began to re-investigate the murder, they succeeded in rebuilding the shattered remains of trust and confidence in the police. They did so, not because they succeeded where their predecessors had failed in convicting the murderers, but by convincing the family and their supporters that they were sincere in their ambition to detect the murderers and appreciated that they needed to win the confidence of the family. It was not *what* the police achieved, but *how* they conducted themselves that mattered.

CHAPTER SUMMARY

It ain't rocket science . . . It's more difficult than that!

Police officers are figures of authority; they intervene in situations where normal life has been gravely disturbed or has broken down entirely; they frequently confront raw emotion; they deal with people whom they would otherwise consider an anathema; they have the capacity to wield great power over the lives of others; yet they are constrained to act disinterestedly and still with compassion, even to those whom they consider utterly obnoxious; and, finally, they do all of this, not on their own territory, but in the streets and in the homes of others. As job specifications go, they rarely come more demanding than this. Policing tests the professionalism of all who are sworn to uphold the highest values of democracy. Like any profession, policing is done by *practitioners* who 'practise' their profession – that is, they walk the talk!

Apart from doing what is right and proper, police who behave professionally in their encounters with the public are putting credit in the bank to draw upon when things go awry, as they inevitably will. The more that people feel that police officers routinely treat them with respect, the more they will reciprocate that respect and give the police the benefit of the doubt.

FURTHER READING

Despite policing being a 'people business', there are no published guides on how this business should be conducted. Perhaps the nearest it comes is in the work of Tom Tyler, especially his and Yuen Huo's *Trust in the Law* (New York: Russell Sage, 2002). It would also be valuable to read the official evaluation report on the National Reassurance Policing Programme by Rachel Tuffin, Julia Morris and Alexis Poole (London: Home Office, 2006), which looks likely to inform police policy for the foreseeable future. Pay particular and critical attention to how reassurance policing makes only a hesitant contribution to reducing crime and disorder. Its major impact is not on outcomes but on process: what residents in the sites selected for the pilot liked so much was that the police were listening to their concerns and endeavouring to do something about them.

One of the reasons for the absence of academic guides is that these are aspects of policing that must be practised. Being self-confident in public places, authoritative but not overbearing in dealings with the public, compassionate and yet sceptical of complaints by victims, all takes a great deal of practice and cannot readily be prescribed.

REFERENCES

Allen, J (2006) *Worry about Crime in England and Wales: Findings from the 2003/04 and 2004/05 British Crime Survey* (Online Report 15/06). London: Research, Development and Statistics Directorate, Home Office.

Corbett, C (2003) *Car Crime*, Cullompton: Willan.

Garland, D (2001) *The Culture of Control: Crime and Social Order in Contemporary Society*. Oxford: Oxford University Press.

Grieve, J (2009) The Stephen Lawrence Inquiry: from intelligence failure to intelligence legacy?, in Hall, N, Grieve, J and Savage, S P (eds) *Policing and the Legacy of Lawrence*. Cullompton: Willan.

Independent Police Complaints Commission (IPCC) (2009) Deaths during or following police contact: statistics for England and Wales 2008/09, in *IPCC Annual Report 2008/09*. London: IPCC.

Kriesi, H (1989) New social movements and the new class in the Netherlands, *American Journal of Sociology*, 94(5): 1078–116.

Sherman, L W, Gottfredson, D, MacKenzie, J, Eck, J, Reuter, P and Bushway, S (1997) *Preventing Crime: What Works, What Doesn't, What's Promising*. Washington, DC: Office of Justice Programs, US Department of Justice.

Skogan, W G (2006) Asymmetry in the impact of encounters with police. *Policing and Society*, 16: 99–126.

Tyler, T R (1990) *Why People Obey the Law*. New Haven, CT: Yale University Press.

Tyler, T R (2004) Enhancing police legitimacy, in Skogan, W G (ed.) *To Better Serve and Protect: Improving Police Practices*, Vol. 593. Beverly Hills, CA: Sage Publications.

Tyler, T R and Huo, Y J (2002) *Trust in the Law: Encouraging Public Cooperation with the Police and Courts*. New York: Russell Sage.

6 Police culture: canteens, carriers and carousing!

CHAPTER OBJECTIVES

By the end of this chapter you should be able to:

- grasp the idea of a 'police culture';
- identify its main characteristics;
- recognise why it is widely regarded as problematic.

Introduction

This chapter will explain what is meant by the 'police culture' and why it is regarded as a malign influence. We will also examine the prospects for changing police culture and offer guidance to a generation of professional police officers in being exposed to such a culture.

What is police culture?

Social scientists have long been fascinated by the question, 'What are the police *really* like?' Pioneering research (Bittner, 1967, 1970, 1974, 1976; Holdaway, 1983; Manning, 1977; Skolnick, 1966) delved into the world that the police occupied and returned to the outside world with accounts of this strange tribe in our midst with their peculiar customs. What was the portrait of police officers that emerged from these expeditions? Like any culture, police culture is composed of beliefs, values and practices that readily describe and explain how and why things happen (few police officers are unable to explain why crime occurs and how it could be dealt with). Police officers have their particular slang and a humour that is wry, if not black. However, there are certain aspects of the police subculture to which researchers and commentators repeatedly return (Reiner, 2000; Waddington, 1999a, 1999b):

- *Mission*: the view of the police is that they are the proverbial 'thin blue line' that stands between anarchy and order (Fielding, 1994). This is a vision that is repeatedly re-affirmed in the police press (such as the regular *Police Review* column, 'Station

Sergeant', which prints a weekly diatribe of authoritarian nostrums worthy of an American 'shock jock' and is worryingly popular among the magazine's readership). The only role that is valued is that of crime-fighting and yet all the evidence indicates that this is a delusion.

PRACTICAL TASK

Read current issues of Police Review *and draw a portrait of how lower-rank officers think and feel. Be careful to avoid official products influenced by press officers!*

- *Action and excitement*: canteen conversation continues to perpetuate the myth that policing is centrally concerned with the 'search, chase and arrest', and officers relish telling 'war stories' that glorify violent encounters. Punch-ups are valorised long after the event. A quarter of a century after it occurred, the policing of the miners' strike continues to echo through police canteens.

- *Cult of masculinity*: despite the huge influx of women police officers that followed the desegregation of policing in the 1970s and the growing ranks of senior women officers, the police retains a resolutely masculine ethos. Women complain that prestigious policing roles (detective work, firearms, riot control) remain unwelcoming to women, who are expected to prove themselves.

- *Us/Them*: the police are notoriously insular, distinguishing between 'Us' (the police) and 'Them' (the rest of the population). The attitude towards 'Us' is one of intense peer solidarity and loyalty that is expressed in practice through the eagerness with which officers support colleagues who call for help. 'Rookies' (as Americans call them) need to earn membership of the club, demonstrating allegiance and reliability to their fellows. Officers are often so insular that they are fiercely loyal to their shift or station and dismissive of fellow officers deployed on other shifts or at other stations. However, there is a huge divide between street cops and management cops, in which distrust tends to be mutual.

- *Racism is endemic* (Holdaway, 2007; Holdaway and O'Neill, 2006, 2007): it continues to erupt in scandals as it did in the Macpherson Inquiry (Macpherson of Cluny et al., 1999) and the covert television documentary *The Secret Policeman*, in which police recruits were seen expressing grotesquely racist views.

- *Authoritarian conservativism*: police officers continue to hold and express authoritarian conservative attitudes, for instance in relation to gay rights.

- *Suspicion and cynicism*: police officers have a distinctively jaundiced view of the world. It is expressed in the distinctively black humour of the police towards normally distressing events such as sudden death. Needless to say, such cynicism is also expressed in opposition to police reforms such as community policing. Such cynicism takes a more sinister turn when it is directed towards the criminal justice process, where the principal concern is not to pursue propriety, but to secure conviction while 'covering your back'.

Why is it a problem?

It is not, we hope you agree, a flattering portrayal, but let us get it into perspective. Similarly unflattering portrayals could be distilled from the libraries of academic research on other professions. Yet, academic research on the cultures of these other occupations has not seeped into the public domain with the damaging consequences that research on the 'canteen culture' of the police has had. Most notable was the Macpherson Report into the murder of Stephen Lawrence (Macpherson of Cluny et al., 1999), which pinned the label 'institutional racism' on the police and sent the morale of officers spiralling into decline. What crucially justified this label was the racial disproportionality of stop and search, which at the time of the inquiry amounted to Black people being five times over-represented among those stopped and searched.

As we have already noted, police work relies heavily upon discretion exercised by police officers, especially in resorting to their legal powers. We have also noted that this amounts to a tremendous investment of trust in the police by citizens who expect their rights to be respected. However, on what does discretion rely? It should be founded upon an expectation that officers use their powers in good faith and *not maliciously – discretion relies on personal integrity.* So, when, as happened during the Macpherson Inquiry, officers repeatedly use anachronistic and offensive words to describe ethnic minorities – describing Stephen Lawrence as 'coloured' – the Inquiry team were left to conclude that there was at best a fundamental gulf between the police and the ethnic minority communities they policed. When that gulf is reinforced by representatives of the National Black Police Association complaining of the routine racism that pervades the police; evidence of such racism from a procession of successful cases brought before industrial tribunals; and representations from official equality organisations supported by academic researchers, it is easy to see how the disparities in rates of stop and search would lead to 'a clear core conclusion of racist stereotyping'.

One might object that the conclusion of the Inquiry was flawed: when discretion is limited by descriptions of witnesses and victims, rather than being exercised solely by the officer relying on intuition, racial disproportionality in stop and search increases rather than decreases, suggesting that ordinary members of the public point the finger of accusation at ethnic minorities even more than the police (FitzGerald, 1999); or when compared, not to the resident population, but to the racial profile of people in public places where they are available to be stopped and searched, patterns of stop and search correspond closely to that profile (MVA and Miller, 2000; Waddington et al., 2004); or that, compared to educational failure and school exclusions, the disparities exhibited by the police are less disadvantageous to ethnic minorities and are being more vigorously tackled by the police (Rollock, 2009). While all this is true, it is irrelevant: the police were discredited not least by revelations about their private conduct towards fellow officers.

The Macpherson Inquiry was undoubtedly a disaster for the police, but other professions have suffered what seem on the face of things to have been far greater potential disasters without causing a comparable impact on their credibility. For instance, the medical profession played host to one of the *world's* most predatory serial murderers – Harold Shipman (Smith, 2005). Nor was Shipman a solitary example – there has been a series of cases in which doctors and, more commonly, nurses have been found guilty of killing their patients. More recently, the Healthcare Commission found that standards of care in the Staffordshire Hospital Trust were so chronically low that many patients needlessly died as a result. The Audit Commission (2005) estimates that the annual rate of fatal medical accidents may be as high as 32,000, which leaves the 92 deaths following police contact of any kind (IPCC, 2009) looking puny by comparison. Yet, the *integrity* of the medical profession has not been impugned.

There is good reason why deaths at the hands of medical practitioners do not arouse concerns comparable to deaths at the hands of the police, and that is *force*. If a doctor or nurse causes the death of a patient, we can reasonably presume that they were at least trying to help the person – they were providing a service, however mistakenly. When people die at the hands of the police, it is usually because the police are inflicting treatment that the recipient does not desire. Forty of the aforementioned deaths in custody arose from traffic collisions, 22 of which occurred during pursuits where drivers were trying to escape and police were trying to prevent them. All but three of these deaths were of those who were occupants of the pursued vehicle. One is entitled to ask who is responsible for such deaths.

On the one hand, one might take the view that drivers should comply with the law that obliges them to stop when required to do so by a police officer and that, if they seek to escape, the responsibility for any death or injury they suffer should be theirs. On the other hand, many commentators ask whether the fatal consequences of pursuing those who escape is commensurate with the reasons for stopping them, for the decision to *pursue* is *discretionary*. Again, one might ask whether there are alternative methods of stopping vehicles under more controlled conditions that diminish the likelihood of a fatal collision. Some worry that the thrill of chase may be what encourages police officers to pursue vehicles, rather than any cool calculation of whether the pay-off is worth the risk.

In sum, because policing is *not* a service that those who come into the hands of the police wish to receive (as is medicine), but is instead *imposed by force*, it inevitably makes policing such a questionable activity in any democracy.

There is currently much talk in policing circles about 'reassurance policing', which relies upon the notion that the police must be *seen* to address the issues that local people bring to the attention of the police. This is a positive and welcome development, but if the police view it as simply a strategy for addressing problems beyond themselves, they will not exploit it to the full. The public wants and needs constant reassurance that the police are exercising their considerable discretionary powers correctly. This reassurance becomes particularly valuable when police commit positive errors, as they inevitably will. The police need desperately to be able to turn to the community and say, 'OK, we got it wrong, but you know we're regular guys who try our best to get it right.'

Suggestions that leak out of the canteen of bawdy, sexist, racist, homophobic and other discreditable attitudes and behaviour erode confidence. When the police say, as they might have done in the case of the Stephen Lawrence murder, 'We tried our best to find the perpetrators. Sorry, we failed', ethnic minorities are entitled to wonder whether that failure was simply the result of police not trying hard enough because of what they have heard about endemic racism within the force.

Can it be changed?

There have been numerous attempts to change police culture among different police organisations in different jurisdictions, with varying results. When the police try to change the culture directly, as did the Metropolitan Police in the early 1990s with the 'Plus programme' (following a report from management consultants, Wolffe Olins), results are very modest at best. This is because, while culture includes intellectual aptitudes, such as beliefs, perceptions, attitudes, emotions and the like, these do not inhabit an isolated universe. Common experience shows us how difficult it is to change attitudes by appealing to the person to see sense and alter their views. Even in the marketing of commercial products, the phenomenon of brand loyalty shows us that people are very resistant to changing their favourite brand of cornflakes, even when the only difference between this brand and any other is the box in which the cornflakes arrive! Consider how soccer supporters remain vehemently supportive of a team whose players are bought and sold like commodities, and a player who in one season is revered by fans as a saviour may be despised in later seasons as someone who betrayed their loyalty by moving to a rival club!

Hence, when the police try really hard to change their culture, they either try to select recruits with suitable attitudes or commit themselves to a sustained training regime. The problem with selecting recruits with suitable subjective characteristics is that no one is sure what those subjective characteristics should be. Like any other occupation, and more than most, policing requires a broad repertoire of attributes that can be invoked in different circumstances. A compassionate police officer would be suitable for notifying the bereaved of the loss of their loved one, but someone of more callous temperament might be more useful at the scene of an accident in which body parts need to be recovered. However, it is highly likely that a roads policing officer would be called upon to perform both duties, sometimes in very quick succession.

Training has not faired any better. For those who believe in the power of training, the most depressing case study is that meticulously researched by Professor Janet Chan (1997, 2003). The circumstances were as favourable to progressive reform of police culture as they are ever likely to be: the reforms took place in the aftermath of a major scandal that had discredited the New South Wales police; a 'white knight' was appointed to introduce thoroughgoing community policing reforms; John Avery, the new commissioner, had a long-established reputation for commitment to liberal, community policing; he surrounded himself with senior officers who were also committed; the training programme for recruits was completely overhauled and officers involved in it were completely in tune with the new regime; and the recruits were among the brightest and the best of their generation, comprising both men and women and diverse ethnicities.

By the completion of their initial period of training, the recruits wholeheartedly subscribed to the values that they had been taught. While on their field training, they were entrusted to carefully vetted supervisors who also adhered to the community policing ethic. To the surprise and dismay of the officers responsible for designing and implementing this training regime, upon their return from field training, recruits had switched from being champions of community police values to become indistinguishable from their hard-bitten, cynical, traditional officers (Chan, 2003).

It is instructive to consider Chan's explanation for the failure of this reform process (Chan, 1997), because she locates it not within the officers themselves, nor the police taken in isolation, but in the character of New South Wales itself, especially its colonial history, which has imprinted upon contemporary social relations deep fissures between Aboriginal peoples and post-colonial immigrants. In other words, the job the recruits (and all other NSW police officers) were asked to do was a far more powerful influence than anything that the training school could deliver.

However, there is a serious weakness in Chan's position, because what is so remarkable about police culture is its consistency, both over time and from one place to another. There are differences, but they are almost exclusively variations upon a theme (Waddington, 1999b). A recent international research project has reaffirmed the near-universality of the police culture (Waddington et al., 2009). Focus groups of police officers in England, the Netherlands, Germany, Australia, Venezuela and Brazil were presented with a virtually identical three-stage scenario that commenced with two local youths being stopped regarding a minor traffic offence, which developed through the recognition of one of them as a small-time criminal, the detection of cannabis smoke within the car, and a drive-off with a high-speed chase, into an armed encounter.

There was a huge difference between the South American police and their colleagues in Europe and Australia, because the South Americans felt almost certain that there would be a 'shoot-out' in these circumstances, whereas the others felt that this was a very remote possibility – a difference that corresponds closely to much higher rates of police shootings in South America compared to the other countries represented. Almost as interesting is that, apart from language differences, members of all the focus groups were expressing very similar attitudes, for example regarding their appraisal of the two youths. What distinguished the South Americans was a real and justified appraisal of the threat that the officers in the scenario would be facing in real-life circumstances.

Where we agree with Chan is in locating the source of police culture, not within officers, but within the job that they do. However, since the surface layers of policing are very different (as across the six jurisdictions covered by the scenario research), whatever it is that drives police culture must be some deeply immutable core. We maintain that that core is the capacity to use violence against fellow citizens. This is an extraordinary power, especially when invested in younger and less experienced members of the police and of society. A police officer has the authority to arrest the Prime Minister if the latter is reasonably suspected of a crime (although we don't offer this as a career-enhancing opportunity!). It weighs heavily and so it should.

Dealing with police culture

So what does the aspiring *professional* police officer do in these circumstances? First of all, get the situation in perspective. Police culture can change, and has done so: following the Macpherson report, there has been a marked decline in some of the more offensive manifestations of racism, albeit that other unsavoury attitudes (sexism and homophobia) continue to be expressed (Foster et al., 2005). It is a small change, but one for the better.

Second, recognise the talk and actions of colleagues for what they are. The canteen and personnel carrier act as stages on which people who are, as often you will be, scared, revolted and emotionally overwhelmed, but present to their colleagues a competent and self-confident image (Fielding, 1984, 1988); they are most definitely *not* 'telling it like it is'! In an intellectually courageous book that aroused feminist indignation, Carolyn Hoyle contrasted how police officers *talk* and *act* regarding accusations of domestic violence. She found a marked contrast: asked about domestics, officers were contemptuous; but when faced with actual circumstances of domestic violence, they were far more often considerate, cared about the safety of mothers and children, and willingly took risks to arrest men who they believed were terrorising their own families (Hoyle, 1998). The problem is that care and consideration does not really 'cut it' in the canteen.

Third, you must appreciate who and what you are as a graduate of a vocational policing degree. This is tantamount to the injection of women and ethnic minorities into the police in earlier generations. Yes, you will be viewed with hostility, especially by officers who consider you and others who are entering the police much better qualified than they were at a comparable stage of their careers. Appreciate that: it is, in itself, part of the test of your professionalism. In the canteen and other such stages do not be tempted to join in and compete for prestige and respect, for that is of passing significance. Neither should you attract the attention of others; quiet understatement is always a better strategy than vocal affirmation of difference. Recognise that you will be tested by other officers and make it clear that you are not willing to 'take the examination' they have set. Uphold your professional values and eventually you will be appreciated for what you *do* on the streets and elsewhere in your professional capacity, as were previous generations of female officers who were similarly tested and triumphed against ingrained misogyny.

It is also important *not* to imagine that everyone will be hostile, or that the hostility shown in the canteen is any more than strutting on a stage. Among your colleagues there will be many who aspire to be professional police officers and it would be wise to affiliate with them. More importantly, there will be very many officers who, despite what they say in the canteen, perform their policing duties with consummate professionalism. Learn from them, for most of policing is a *craft*, not a science, and like any other craft it must be *practised*. Therefore, you must be open to what is good practice and seek to learn from it, while refusing to accept poor or bad practice.

Pioneering is always an arduous way to go, for by definition pioneers chart their own course. On the other hand, pioneers are able to grab any benefits of being first!

CHAPTER SUMMARY

In this chapter we have tried to alert you to the seductive allure of police culture. Professionalism in the police is a very personal issue: it is one of adhering to the values of public service, integrity and honesty, when all around there are temptations to divert from those values. At the same time, it is vitally important that you do not dismiss colleagues who are tempted to diverge from the path of professionalism, but to understand why they do so and find alternative solutions to the problems that all police officers confront. This is a challenge, for it requires creative imagination within the parameters of remaining professional. Well, no one (we hope) promised you a rose garden!

FURTHER READING

In Australia, Professor Janet Chan has challenged some of the basic assumptions on police culture in her article 'Changing police culture' (*British Journal of Criminology*, 1996). This article prompted a recently published collection of essays, *Police Occupational Culture* by Megan O'Neill, Monique Marks and Anne-Marie Singh, which tries to achieve a less censorious approach to police culture and is worth reading (Oxford: Elsevier, 2007).

REFERENCES

Audit Commission (2005) *A Safer Place for Patients: Learning to Improve Patient Safety* (HC 456). London: Audit Commission.

Bittner, E (1967) The police on skid-row: a study of peace keeping. *American Sociological Review*, 32(5): 699–715.

Bittner, E (1970) *The Functions of the Police in a Modern Society*, Washington, DC: US Government Printing Office.

Bittner, E (1974) Florence Nightingale in pursuit of Willie Sutton: a theory of the police, in Jacob, H (ed.) *Potential for Reform of Criminal Justice*. Beverly Hills, CA: Sage.

Bittner, E (1976) Policing juveniles: the social context of common practice, in Rosenheim, M K (ed.) *Pursuing Justice for the Child*, Chicago, IL: Chicago University Press.

Chan, J B L (1996) Changing police culture. *British Journal of Criminology*, 36: 109–34.

Chan, J B L (1997) *Changing Police Culture: Policing in a Multicultural Society*, Cambridge: Cambridge University Press.

Chan, J B L (2003) *Fair Cop: Learning the Art of Policing*, Toronto: University of Toronto Press.

Fielding, N (1984) Police socialization and police competence. *British Journal of Sociology*, 35(4): 568–90.

Fielding, N (1988) *Joining Forces: Police Training, Socialization, and Occupational Competence*. London: Routledge.

Fielding, N (1994) Cop canteen culture, in Newburn, T and Stanko, E (eds) *Just Boys Doing Business: Men, Masculinity and Crime*, London: Routledge.

FitzGerald, M (1999) *Final Report into Stop and Search*. London: Metropolitan Police Authority.

Foster, J, Newburn, T and Souhami, A (2005) *Assessing the Impact of the Stephen Lawrence Inquiry* (Home Office Research Study 294). London: Home Office Research, Development and Statistics Directorate.

Holdaway, S (1983) *Inside the British Police*, Oxford: Blackwell.

Holdaway, S (2007) Institutional racism, in Newburn, T (ed.) *Dictionary of Policing*, Cullompton: Willan.

Holdaway, S and O'Neill, M (2006) Institutional racism after Macpherson: an analysis of police views, *Policing And Society*, 16: 349–69.

Holdaway, S and O'Neill, M (2007) Where has all the racism gone? Views of racism within constabularies after Macpherson. *Ethnic and Racial Studies*, 30: 397–415.

Hoyle, C (1998) *Negotiating Domestic Violence*. Oxford: Clarendon.

Independent Police Complaints Commission (IPCC) (2009) Deaths during or following police contact: statistics for England and Wales 2008/09, in *IPCC Annual Report 2008/09*. London: IPCC.

Macpherson of Cluny, S W, advised by Cook, T, Sentamu, T and Stone, R (1999) *The Stephen Lawrence Inquiry* (Cm 4262-I). London: HMSO.

Manning, P K (1977) *Police Work*. Cambridge, MA: MIT Press.

MVA Consultancy and Miller, J (2000) *Profiling Populations Available for Stops and Searches* (Police Research Series Paper 131). London: Policing and Reducing Crime Unit, Research, Development and Statistics Directorate, Home Office.

O'Neill, M, Marks, M and Singh, A-M (eds) (2007) *Police Occupational Culture: New Debates and Directions*. Sociology of Crime, Law and Deviance, Vol 8. Amsterdam: Elsevier.

Reiner, R (2000) *The Politics of the Police*, 3rd edition. Oxford: Oxford University Press.

Rollock, N (2009) Education policy and the impact of the Lawrence Inquiry: the view from another sector, in Hall, N, Grieve, J and Savage, S P (eds) *Policing and the Legacy of Lawrence*. Cullompton: Willan.

Skolnick, J H (1966) *Justice Without Trial*. New York: Wiley.

Smith, Dame J (2005) *Shipman: the Final Report* (Sixth Report of The Shipman Inquiry). London: Crown Copyright.

Waddington, P A J (1999a) Police (canteen) sub-culture: an appreciation. *British Journal of Criminology*, 39(2): 286–308.

Waddington, P A J (1999b) *Policing Citizens*. London: UCL Press.

Waddington, P A J, Stenson, K and Don, D (2004) In proportion: race, and police stop and search. *British Journal of Criminology*, 44(6): 889–914.

Waddington, P A J, Adang, O, Baker, D, Birkbeck, C, Feltes, T, Gabaldón, L G, Paes Machado, E and Stenning, P (2009) Singing the same tune? International continuities and discontinuities in how police talk about using force. *Crime, Law and Social Change*, 52 (Special issue on *Policing Talk About the Use of Force: A Comparative International Perspective*): 111–38.

7 Wrongdoing and accountability

CHAPTER OBJECTIVES

By the end of this chapter you should be able to:

- recognise the inherent temptations that policing provides for committing wrongdoing;
- appreciate how small and apparently inconsequential steps can lead to serious wrongdoing;
- recognise the importance of how policing perpetually involves proverbially walking along the 'invitational edges of corruption';
- understand how ineffectual rules are against wrongdoing;
- grasp the importance of personal integrity as a shield against temptation;
- understand how complaints against individual wrongdoing are dealt with;
- comprehend how the police as an organisation is held accountable;
- appreciate how external events can have a profound impact on police policy and the lives and careers of individual officers;
- recognise that professionalism is a robust defence against hostile scrutiny;
- acknowledge the dangers of police being seen to 'police themselves'.

Introduction

In this chapter we deal with one of the most important, yet sensitive, issues in policing: wrongdoing by officers and mechanisms to prevent it.

Bent coppers

Police officers behave as badly as anyone: some of them cheat the taxman, others steal, a few kill. Every occupation suffers from members who commit criminal actions. Yet there is something special about police officers who lie, cheat and steal, because sometimes they do so as part of their job. We return to the fundamental professional issue of policing – officers perform as duties actions that would otherwise be exceptional, exceptionable or *downright illegal*. Sometimes, they use the cover of 'duty' to engage in actual illegality.

Areas of corruption

Wrongdoing manifests itself repeatedly in three aspects of police work: bribery and corruption; denial of civil and human rights; and the use of force.

Bribery and corruption

Americans call it 'graft' – misusing discretion to allow criminality to continue in return for some reward. At the bottom end of the scale, it might mean overlooking technical violations, such as vehicles parking in a no-parking zone to off-load produce to retailers, who then give handsome discounts to police officers on anything bought at the respective stores. Rarely is anything said about this, but often commercial undertakings of various sorts are known to be GTP (Good to Police).

The problem becomes more severe when the commercial undertakings in question are engaged in crime, most commonly vice and drugs. In the past, many vice and drug offences were regarded by criminologists as 'crimes without victims', but more recently they and most people have become aware that there are many victims associated with these activities. For instance, the women, and sometimes children, who are compelled to perform sex acts for money are often direct victims, as are the users of illegal drugs. There are victims in a wider sense too: those who live in areas blighted by kerb-crawlers and drug abusers anxious to steal anything they can sell to raise funding for their habit.

Pro- and reactive policing

The description 'crimes without victims' points to two very important features of vice and drugs (and perhaps some other crimes). First, those most directly involved in vice and drugs offences rarely complain about their victimisation, at least in respect of their vice and drug-taking activities – although they often complain about other things. For instance, the client of a prostitute is unlikely to complain to the police that the prostitute gave inadequate service, and neither is the drug taker likely to complain about the quality of the drug that has been supplied. This has a vitally important effect on how these offences are policed: if there are few, if any, complainants, policing cannot be reactive (that is, following up complaints in the normal manner). Therefore, if the police are to do anything about these crimes, they must do it *proactively*, that is, on their own initiative. That means identifying targets and gathering evidence of their illicit activity, both of which tend to bring officers into close contact with offenders, either as undercover officers who might present themselves as consumers of the illicit service being offered, or through cultivating informants.

Crime as a business

The other aspect to which crimes without victims draws our attention is that vice and drugs are both conducted as businesses, however small these enterprises may be. They are sellers in a market in which there are buyers who willingly consume their service or products. Like any entrepreneur, the illicit trader will try to ensure the most favourable market conditions, for example by excluding competitors from the most profitable trading locations. Police activity places a restriction on the ability to trade profitably, so illicit businesses try to do what their legitimate counterparts frequently do, that is, 'regulatory capture'. For example, it is fairly common for those who have occupied positions of power and influence in regulatory authorities, including ministers and state officials, to be offered lucrative positions in the corporations they previously regulated – a case of gamekeeper turned poacher! Illicit businesses do the same by attempting to bring their 'regulators' (the police) on to the 'board of directors' and paying them accordingly, that is, they bribe them. When huge profits are being made by vice and drug entrepreneurs, they are in a position to tempt officers with money, or seduce them into compromising situations (for example, using prostitutes or consuming drugs). The services supplied by those involved in vice and drugs are intrinsically seductive – that is why consumers become 'hooked'.

Hence, it should come as little surprise that repeatedly police officers, squads or entire organisations can find themselves subverted by drugs and vice entrepreneurs.

Civil and human rights

The police routinely deal with people from whom most others would recoil: smelly, disease-ridden, alcoholic vagrants; drug abusers and prostitutes; families living the most appallingly disorganised lives; child abusers and paedophiles, and so on. Apart from this, the police deal with ordinary people who are at the 'end of their tethers', who are unable to cope and highly emotional, and who turn, often in desperation, to the police. Police officers often use derogatory slang to describe this section of the population: 'toe-rags', 'scumbags', 'slags' and so on. They also pick up the pieces of those who have been victimised (who are often the very same people as described above) and encounter the reality of lives shattered by crime. Yet all these folk are citizens who enjoy rights. Not the least of these are suspects and there is the danger that officers do not regard suspects as deserving of the rights they are afforded and employ various tactics to circumvent or deny rights.

The temptation to violate rights becomes hugely increased in high-profile cases where there is public, media and political pressure to detect a horrific crime. A terrorist tactic is to commit an outrage that provokes an overreaction and thus inflicts physical damage and simultaneously undermines the legitimacy of the state. The reputation of the British police was gravely undermined by the cases of the Birmingham Six, the Guildford Four and other cases associated with Irish republican terrorism during the 1970s that produced a set of miscarriages of justice. These scandals impeded the effectiveness of counter-terrorism, exposing the public to further attack.

Use of force

Police are entrusted with the monopoly of sovereign state force, which means that they grapple, struggle, fight and use weapons (batons, CS spray and possibly guns). Like anyone else in such circumstances, the sympathetic nervous system is excited – the 'fight or flight' response – and it is sometimes tempting to use violence gratuitously, especially against those regarded by officers as undeserving of more gentle treatment. In public order situations, officers might find themselves confronting hostile gatherings, among whom there may be those who hurl missiles at police cordons, or who at closer quarters spit or squirt noxious fluids. The temptation is to lash out in response, especially if there is a baton charge to clear an area. In armed operations, officers may be highly charged and primed to see and respond instantly to suspicious movements.

Invitational edges of corruption

One of the foremost pioneers of police research pointed to the intrinsic features of policing that actively invite breaching the rules. He called these occasions the 'invitational edges of corruption' (Manning, 1997), but criminologists have long pointed out that delinquency of all kinds tends to be a 'drift' (Matza, 1969) rather than a clear break.

'You can't police according to the book'

Police officers in all those jurisdictions where research has been done are prone to utter this phrase. They are correct – if police officers complied strictly with the law and codes of conduct, they would bring society to a halt. Sometimes they do so deliberately as a means of exerting pressure on employers during labour disputes – in the USA it is known as a 'ticket blizzard'. Rules must be implemented with discretion and this is a vitally important and valuable role that the police perform. Rules must also be interpreted, because rules are necessarily written as generalities, whereas they are invariably applied to specific circumstances.

The invitation to corruption lies at the point of discretion and interpretation. This is even more so when we consider not the law, but evidence, because 'What happened?' in confused, chaotic and ambiguous circumstances is often far from clear and only becomes so upon reflection. However, is that reflection actually construction? Psychology has demonstrated how everyone seeks coherence and meaning, which is imposed upon events rather than residing in them. If an officer is engaged in a struggle with a suspect from which they emerge with a bruise, it is obvious that the bruise was caused by the suspect, rather than perhaps being the result of an accidental collision with an object.

None of this is, in itself, wrongdoing. It is simply how rules are applied to actual cases. However, it creates an 'invitational edge', for there is little difference at the margin between the interpretation of what happened and the manufacture of evidence. For example, if drugs are found near to where a suspect was standing, it is tempting to construe this as the suspect having been seen to *drop* them. The temptation to take this tiny, but fateful, step is increased when the suspect is a well-known drug user (evidence that would not be admissible in court). A further temptation is to insert a small element so as to satisfy rules of evidence.

To catch a thief

A young officer on plain-clothes work was keeping observation near some commercial premises. The police had information that the premises were to be broken into. It was a summer night and they expected that the break-in would take place after dark. The officer was working with a colleague with whom he was in radio contact.

They had been keeping watch on the premises for about three hours when he heard a disturbance behind a fence in the garden from where he was keeping watch. A man climbed over the fence and went towards the commercial building. The officer then lost sight of him. He called up his colleague on the radio and told him what was happening, but continued to keep watch. Shortly afterwards, there was a commotion from near the building and a person came crashing through the undergrowth and fencing in the adjoining gardens, behind the fence from which the first man had come. The officer decided to give chase to this second person. By the time he had climbed over the fences, the person had got away.

The officer then went to help his colleague and found him struggling with the first man. Together, they subdued him and took him out into the adjacent road, which had street lighting. The man started to struggle again but they managed to contact the police control room for transport. When they got back to the police station, the officer who had been in the garden dealt with the prisoner, searched him and placed him in a cell. His colleague went back to the scene of the observation with a sergeant. When they returned, they said they had found a window broken at the rear of the commercial premises. As a result, the more experienced officer charged the prisoner with burglary.

This surprised the officer, but he waited until he could speak to his colleague in private. He told him that he was sure he would have heard the sound of glass breaking if the man had actually got that far. Was it old damage? His colleague said, 'You are being naive. We are not letting him get away with that. There has to be a broken window. Just leave it at that.'

(Source: Adapted extract from Wright and Irving, 1996)

'Not *really* a crime, is it?'

One of the temptations when dealing with 'crimes without victims' is to regard the activity as 'not really a crime'. It has already been mentioned that vice and drugs are illicit markets, where suppliers and customers willingly transact deals. So who is harmed?

It is a legal and moral domain that is fluid: photographs of naked women that, within living memory, would have shocked and appalled most people may, a generation later, be commonplace. So, who is to say what is immoral and depraved?

Among some migrant groups it is perfectly normal for elders to arrange marriages for the young, who may have little or no say in the matter. Is this forced marriage? When do influence and expectation become force (Gangoli and McCarry, 2008)?

Neither is this restricted to the fringes of vice and drugs. At the serious end of the spectrum, the Serious Organised Crime Agency examines major drugs and other illicit trafficking (arms and migrants), fraudulent scams, and the activities of criminal networks

(Harfield, 2006). What they do not pay attention to are health and safety violations. Why not? Is it not serious that health and safety violations cause thousands of injuries to workers every year, some hundreds of which prove fatal (Tombs et al., 2006)? Is it not organised when brewing companies conspire with local authorities to transform town and city high streets into oases of alcohol-fuelled violence (Hadfield, 2006)?

Perhaps most striking of all is the abject failure of the police to enforce speed limits on roads. Speed is the killer in most serious traffic collisions, and yet not only does traffic routinely exceed speed limits, attempts by some brave Chief Constables to impose zero tolerance are successfully resisted by the mobilisation of the motoring public (Corbett, 2003).

The arbitrariness with which the law is enforced engenders within police officers a tacit relativism that tends to shift attention away from *what* has been done and towards *who* did it? Largely, this means avoiding the crimes of the powerful and respectable, and bearing down heavily on the powerless and disadvantaged; the usual suspects of young, ill-educated, lower-class, ethnic-minority men – what Choongh (1998) refers to, using the slang of the police officers he observed, as 'dross'. Arbitrariness is difficult to reconcile with vocation and so it is tempting to convince oneself that it is the young, foul-mouthed, aggressive drunk staggering around in the middle of the road who is 'the problem' and not those responsible for the pub out of which he has staggered. Having convinced oneself, it is easy to regard such a person as undeserving of the rights of citizenship.

The cup of coffee problem

Things were much simpler in an earlier era, when the police were transferred with sufficient regularity to ensure that they formed no attachments to any of those who resided or worked in the area covered by their beat. Fraternising was definitely forbidden, and stern sergeants were known to creep around, seeking constables who supped a cup of tea with kindly residents (Brogden, 1991; Weinberger, 1995). What was once fraternising is today community policing, but why did an earlier generation of senior police officers strictly forbid what today is encouraged? The answer is: the 'cup of coffee problem' (Feldberg, 1985). If police form allegiances with those whom they police, the general social rule that one should reciprocate (for instance, buying one's round of drinks) becomes a temptation to stray towards the invitational edge.

Suppose officers receive hospitality at a local vehicle repair shop. When later they attend road traffic accidents, they might recommend the repair shop. They may do so in good faith, for they have seen the workmanship produced in the repair shop. What if now the grateful repair shop proprietor offers to repair the officers' vehicles at reduced cost; have the officers strayed into a compromising relationship? Certainly, that was seen as a danger, and procedures were adopted for tow trucks to be allocated by control rooms unsullied by such fraternising.

That recognises the problem, but does not extinguish it. Cups of coffee are not only consumed by community police officers. Senior officers are frequently members of the 'rubber chicken circuit' – that is, the lunches held by various associations, often involving prominent local business people. The purpose of many of these 'rubber chicken' lunches is to facilitate informal communication, which for business people may allow commercial opportunities to be initiated and pursued. It also facilitates business people bringing their concerns to the attention of the police. To the extent that these people are persuasive (and why bother if they are not?), senior officers will use their discretion to pay more attention to some problems than others. Criminologists have long pointed out that policing selectively pays attention to the 'crime in the streets' not the 'crime in the suites', and it is not difficult to see why.

CASE STUDY

The smartest guys in the room

Enron was a vast and vastly wealthy corporation founded in 1985, which by the 1990s was fêted as one of the most innovative large companies in the USA, according to Fortune's 'Most Admired Companies' survey. It owned and operated gas pipelines, electricity plants, pulp and paper plants, broadband assets and water plants internationally, and traded in financial markets for the same products and services. Its share price was buoyant: at the end of 2000 its market capitalisation was a staggering $60 billion. However, much of this wealth had more to do with financial engineering than engineering for oil, gas or any other commodity. Executives set up a dense network of shell companies owned by Enron, but to whom any risk could be attributed. When trading conditions turned in an unfavourable direction, Enron executives used this impenetrable network as a shield behind which to shelter fraudulently.

Eventually, the whole edifice collapsed like a pack of cards and, by the end of 2001, Enron filed for bankruptcy in Europe and then the USA. It cost 4,000 employees their jobs, and 15,000 employees held 60+ per cent of their savings in Enron stock, which became worthless overnight. The Chairman of Enron, Kenneth Lay, and Chief Executive Officer, Jeffrey Skilling, were found guilty of multiple business offences, but Lay died before being sentenced, while Skilling was sentenced to 24 years and four months in prison. It did not stop there: the international firm of accountants, Arthur Andersen, collapsed and severe damage was suffered by Wall Street firms who had Enron as a prominent corporate client.

PRACTICAL TASK

Crime in the suites

Search the internet to find out what you can about any one of the following:

- *Union Carbide, Bophal disaster;*
- *Herald of Free Enterprise, ferry sinking in Zeebrugge harbour;*
- *Piper Alpha oil-rig fire;*
- *Marchioness pleasure-boat disaster;*
- *Bernard Madoff;*
- *BAE corruption.*

Write a brief summary for discussion.

Closing ranks

Why is so little of this more widely understood? The answer is that the culture of policing is solidaristic; it has to be, for otherwise police officers would find it enormously difficult to do their legitimate work. The whole point of Manning's concept of invitational edges is to highlight how the potential for corruption is insinuated into normal, proper, everyday policing. However, the word 'edge' suggests more of a break than is accurate, for it is more a matter of an 'invitational slippery slope'. Even actions taken in the best of good faith can return to haunt police officers.

CASE STUDY

Tony Lundy

Tony Lundy was a conspicuously successful detective in the Metropolitan Police, responsible for many convictions of armed robbers. His reputation was founded on his uncanny ability to convince senior denizens of the 'underworld' to give evidence against their former accomplices. They became known as 'supergrasses', because to 'grass' is to disclose information of wrongdoing among one's personal acquaintances and 'super' referred to the scale of the criminality they revealed. Among Tony Lundy's most successful supergrasses was Roy Garner, a career criminal who received a total of £500,000 during the early 1980s as rewards for evidence supplied to the police via Lundy.

Then another police squad raided a flat occupied by Nikolaus Chrastny and found 14 million pounds' worth of cocaine. Chrastny also became a supergrass and implicated Roy Garner, who in turn was eventually sentenced to 22 years for drugs importation. Now Lundy was accused of conspiring with Garner, allegations that he staunchly rejected and in respect of which the Crown Prosecution Service confirmed that they had no evidence on which to prosecute him. Nevertheless, he retired prematurely on health grounds with the taint of corruption still lingering.

For a sympathetic and full biography of Tony Lundy, see Short (1992). A briefer and less sympathetic account is included in Morton (1993).

Coppers investigating coppers

The Roman poet, Juvenal, posed the fundamental problem of police corruption when he asked: 'quis custodiet ipsos custodes?' – 'Who guards the guardians?' If one set of police officers investigates the alleged wrongdoing of another set of police officers, the suspicion arises that the investigators will tread lightly. This is for two reasons: first, the police are notable for their solidarity – a perfectly proper sentiment in an occupation that confronts endemic dangers; and, second, those who investigate would doubtless have found themselves in compromising situations similar to those in which the targets of their investigation now find themselves. In other words, they might well feel 'There but for the grace of God go I' and, if they do not, there will be many who will intone 'Let he who is without sin cast the first stone.' It is often opined by officers that any of their fellows who is not currently 'carrying' a complaint is simply not doing their job.

The reality is more brutal, for once a complaint reaches the formal stage, investigators will be painfully aware that it is *they* who are in the spotlight and if they fail to investigate thoroughly, they run the considerable risk of being accused of very serious dereliction of duty, at best. There have been many high-profile cases where police investigators have revealed circumstances that have deeply damaged the police, such as Operation Countryman, which investigated allegations of serious corruption among Metropolitan Police detectives. The investigating officers, in turn, made deeply damaging complaints about non-cooperation on the part of the Met.

Similarly, John Stalker's original investigation into an alleged 'shoot to kill' informal policy among members of the Royal Ulster Constabulary (RUC) was taken over by Her Majesty's Chief Inspector of Constabulary after accusations were made about John Stalker's relationships with local criminals in his home force. If this was an attempt to silence criticism, it certainly backfired, since it only added credence to the original allegations.

Sir John Stevens also conducted a series of investigations regarding alleged collusion between members of the RUC and loyalist terrorists during the terrorist campaign in Northern Ireland, and concluded that the allegations were true. Finally, it was the Kent Police who, through their investigations of complaints brought against the Met. by Mr and Mrs Lawrence, revealed the full extent of the incompetence to which the Macpherson Inquiry drew later attention.

Few other occupations could claim to have inflicted as much damage on their own organisations as have the police upon theirs. This is something of which the police should be proud. It stands as evidence of their unwillingness to be swayed from the truth by loyalty to colleagues. It is also a warning to those who might be tempted to cut corners or engage in more questionable conduct, that they can expect little mercy if their conduct falls under suspicion.

No wonder, then, that in the past police found ways of diverting complainants away from making a complaint in the first instance. Those opportunities have been reduced by the possibility of making complaints directly to the Independent Police Complaints Commission (IPCC), either on one's own initiative or with the help of a third party, such as the Citizens Advice Bureau. Moreover, complaints need not be made by the complainant, for third parties may witness something they believe to be intolerable. However, complaints are often relatively trivial and complainants do not necessarily seek bloody revenge. The installation of 'informal resolution', negotiated between the parties without admission of culpability, has become an alternative to full-blown investigation of complaints, leading to a hearing before a quasi-judicial tribunal. The success or otherwise of these arrangements remains to be evaluated.

Safety systems

The current head of the IPCC, Nick Hardwick, aspires to shift the complaints process away from its current punitive stance towards what is called a 'safety systems' approach. An occupation that is inherently the most dangerous is that of civil aviation and that industry has the enviable achievement of creating one of the safest modes of transport available. They have done so by encouraging everyone associated with the industry – passengers and workers in all corners of the business – to complain with a view to rectifying problems. Hence, air safety organisations throughout the world have created anonymous reporting processes, so that attention can be drawn to problems. Even if those problems arise from individual mistakes or wrongdoing, they may have their roots in systems failures that allowed the individual to act as they did.

The IPCC and its predecessor, the Police Complaints Authority, have paid particular attention to deaths at the hands of the police – in the cells, in traffic collisions and during armed confrontations, in each of which can be discerned a groping towards a systems solution. For instance, one of the most hazardous activities in which the police take part is the high-speed pursuit of vehicles failing to stop. Most of these pursuits are initiated by minor traffic violations, albeit that the drivers of escaping vehicles are usually young, inexperienced, unlicensed and often under the influence of intoxicants, and are frequently driving an uninsured and/or stolen vehicle – in short, they are an accident waiting to happen. The safety systems question that arises is whether pursuing such drivers serves to capture and remove them from the road, or exposes other road users to increased peril. Evidence from the USA indicates that the cessation of all pursuits has no adverse impact on crime rates or the likelihood of failing to stop.

Corporate accountability

It is not only individual officers who are held personally accountable for their actions to an unprecedented extent; it is also the police as an organisation. Thirty years ago the situation could be fairly simply described as the 'tripartite system': the Chief Constable, who represented the police organisation of which he (or, rarely in those days, she) was head; the Police Authority, which was a local body comprising in equal measure elected local authority representatives and magistrates; and, finally, the Home Office. Even then it was messy: the Metropolitan Police had no local representation and some police areas encompassed more than one local authority. The tripartite system was also less balanced than the description might suggest, because the Home Office paid by far the greater share and, therefore, had the greatest say. Also, beneath the surface changes were occurring that progressively strengthened the power of the Home Office. Officers could not be promoted wholly within a single force as they had in an earlier (and, it should be said, more corrupt) era. In order to be appointed as a Chief Officer, it is necessary to have served at a rank above Chief Superintendent in another force. In addition, shortlists for Chief Officer rank needed Home Office approval and this was increasingly linked to satisfactory completion of senior command courses at the *national* Police College at Bramshill, Hampshire. This was designed to break the cosy parochialism of officers rising seamlessly through the ranks within a particular area, but it effectively strengthened the influence of the Home Office.

During the turbulent prime ministership of Margaret Thatcher, policing became a hot political issue and a source of major contention between Labour local authorities and the Home Office. Central government also fell out of love with the police once the inner-city riots and picket-line violence of the early 1980s appeared to have been quelled for good. Central government increasingly saw the police as the last remaining unreformed public service and ministers wanted to improve the efficiency of policing. From this mix emerged a revised format of Police Authorities, in which centrally approved non-political members, who brought specific expertise to the Authorities, comprised half the membership. Meanwhile, the Home Office began to drive the police remotely through the creation of a plethora of targets coupled to threats of direct intervention if individual police areas underperformed. These targets acquired an unsavoury reputation, blamed for distorting policing priorities away from targeting chronic but serious issues and redirecting officers towards making easy arrests that satisfied targets.

In a 2009 Green Paper, the government reversed this policy and vowed to set just one target – that of achieving public satisfaction, supported by local policing pledges and vague ideas about greater public consultation at the level of Basic Command Units. Meanwhile, the Conservative Opposition was flirting with the idea of directly electing local heads of the police on the US model. The irony of this is that this was a dream of 1980s' radicals (Jefferson and Grimshaw, 1984), who imagined that a dose of democracy would make the police kinder, more gentle and less racist. Perhaps it was the success of Mayor Giuliani and his Commissioner of the NYPD, Bill Bratton, in promoting the idea of zero tolerance as an election winner that shifted political perceptions!

Meanwhile, the Home Office increased its influence over the police. In the 1990s, the status of Her Majesty's Inspectorate of Constabulary (HMIC) underwent subtle, but still profound, change. Whereas HMIC had acquired a reputation as a comfortable rest home for retired chief constables, a new cohort consisting of thrusting senior officers, still young enough to have ahead of them careers as Chief Constables of major police areas, were appointed to HMIC. The work of HMIC also shifted away from regular and largely ceremonial annual inspections and became more intrusive examinations of performance, supplemented by thematic inspections of particular pressing issues. In 2008, it was HMIC that promoted the amalgamation of forces so as to close the gap in the resourcing of major incidents. This prompted a campaign of resistance from some Chief Constables and their Police Authorities that proved too powerful and HMIC retreated.

Occasionally, HMIC has conducted special investigations following matters arousing controversy. This occurred after the G20 conference in April 2009, which was accompanied by protests, some of which turned violent and aroused controversy. The HMIC report was just one of several – the House of Commons' Home Affairs Select Committee and the Joint Parliamentary Committee on Human Rights both published reports. However, HMIC not only identified failings, but in its second report pointed to necessary reforms in public-order policing. HMIC was not alone as a central influence for reforms in policing. In 2001, the Home Office established the Police Standards Unit, which was paraded as a driver of improved police performance. However, it failed to make its mark and was eventually swallowed up into the general crime and disorder reduction bureaucracy.

In 2006, the Home Office effectively hived off its Police Department and created a new agency – the National Policing Improvements Agency (NPIA), under a Chief Executive who also held the rank of Chief Constable. This coincided with the then Home Secretary announcing that the Home Office was 'not fit for purpose'. The result is to have created yet another seat at the table: Chief Constable, Police Authority, NPIA and Home Office (which still remains the central funding source).

To match this growth in central government power, Chief Constables were increasingly represented in policy-making by an organisation that was originally regarded as their staff association and was used to negotiate terms and conditions of service – the Association of Chief Police Officers (ACPO). As policing became more politicised, so ACPO and especially its President (a Chief Constable who served for one year in rotation) became increasingly prominent political figures. With the growth of international collaboration, it became evident that there was no single representative of the police of England and Wales (still less the UK as a whole) who could speak authoritatively, so ACPO began to fill such voids and influence policy. In 2003, the Presidency of ACPO became a full-time appointment and was incorporated into the Home Office. Likewise, the newly revamped police authorities formed themselves into an Association of Police Authorities in order to achieve a national voice, albeit one that struggles to make itself heard.

One specific responsibility that the Home Office has shed to a limited degree is the Metropolitan Police. Since its inception, the Met. has been held directly accountable to the Home Office, but as policing became more politically contentious the lack of local control of the Met. throughout the London boroughs came to be seen as increasingly anomalous. With the creation of a Mayor and Assembly for London, the Metropolitan Police Authority (MPA) took responsibility for some of the local functions performed by the Met. However, there have been, and remain, tensions between the Mayor, the Assembly and the MPA.

For example, after the controversial shooting to death of an entirely innocent man (Jean Charles de Menezes), who was mistaken for a wanted terrorist suspect, the Assembly passed a motion of no confidence in the Metropolitan Police Commissioner, Sir Ian Blair, but the MPA affirmed its confidence in the Commissioner. When the Mayoralty passed from Ken Livingstone to Boris Johnson, Sir Ian was told that he did not enjoy the confidence of the Mayor and felt it necessary to resign. His successor was appointed in conditions of intense political tension between the Labour Home Secretary and the Conservative Mayor and this effectively set the precedent that any future Commissioner will need to be acceptable to whoever is Mayor at the time.

PRACTICAL TASK

Know your abbreviations and acronyms

Research on the internet, and in this chapter, the following abbreviations and acronyms and memorise them:

• *ACPO*	• *HMIC*	• *NYPD*
• *NPIA*	• *MPA*	• *IAG*
• *APA*	• *IPCC*	• *PACE*
• *NBPA*		

Influence over policing is not restricted by any means to these constitutional arrangements. Policing is, as we have noted, prone to error, and when errors of great magnitude occur it is not uncommon for some kind of official inquiry to take place, which invariably discovers flaws in police structures, operating procedures and so forth, and attributes blame. Recommendations are made to remedy those flaws and become very influential no matter how ill-considered they might be.

For instance, after Ian Huntley murdered Jessica Chapman and Holly Wells, an Inquiry was established under the chairmanship of Sir Michael Bichard. It focused on how Huntley was able to be employed as a school caretaker after it had emerged that, while living in Humberside, his sexual exploits with under-age girls had come to the attention of local social services and the police, yet this information had not been passed on to the Cambridgeshire Constabulary. This became a startling example of what Professor David Garland has called the 'culture of control' (Garland, 2001) and of how blame is used to prompt policy changes.

It was found that the school that employed Huntley as a caretaker had failed to conduct a background check on him, so any supposed failures in the system of supplying information about the suitability of Huntley were entirely hypothetical. Yet, Sir Michael was appalled that, *had* the school sought a background check, information available to the Humberside police and social services would not have been accessible because of the chaotic state of police intelligence. The police knew of Huntley in connection with three sexual liaisons with girls under age, but none of them had led to a conviction. He was a suspect in a case of rape and the investigating officer recorded his opinion that Huntley was potentially very dangerous. However, this was mere opinion, since someone else was convicted of the rape. Local social services also knew of Huntley in respect of other sexual liaisons of a similar kind, but neither agency knew that the other held incriminating information.

Huntley then disappeared from view, to reappear in Soham, where he now was in a steady relationship with Maxine Carr, who became a teaching assistant at the school where Jessica and Holly were pupils and whom she came to know. So far as the Inquiry could discern, Huntley's fatal contact with the two girls was an entirely isolated episode and opportunistic on his part. He had no previous record of violence, nor any convictions, so, if the school had requested a background check, what could that have produced? It would have revealed allegations of sexual misconduct with young girls when he was in his teens, none of which led to conviction and one of which (the rape) was definitely erroneous.

However, to ensure that this extremely rare event should not recur, Sir Michael recommended the creation of a centralised computer system linking not only all police, but also social services. In other words, a centralised intelligence database has been created on which will be stored any amount of tittle-tattle and gossip. That this should be happening at the same time as the DNA database is being legally challenged on the grounds that it is wrong to retain samples taken from those unconvicted of crimes is utterly bizarre, but a powerful example of how vulnerable policing policy has become to wayward events.

It is not only exceptional events that license ill-considered interventions from bodies external to the police. In the early 1990s, and for reasons that remain obscure, the Audit Commission turned its attention to the police, publishing a succession of reports on a wide range of police activity. They proved influential. Let us consider one of these reports, *Streetwise* (Audit Commission, 1996), which authoritatively asserted what most academics had long been aware of, namely that police patrol had little or no discernible impact on levels of crime. From this observation, the authors leapt to the conclusion that there was no point in routine patrol and advanced the mantra of 'intelligence-led policing'. This was not an unwelcome intervention to many senior police officers and it was embraced, albeit rhetorically rather than in actuality, since the public's demand for response policing remained insatiable. A dozen years later, with crime down to levels not seen for decades, the 'reassurance gap' was discovered and the need for the routine presence of uniformed officers in neighbourhoods was reasserted. No apology has yet been received from the Audit Commission; indeed, the author of the report was elevated to the ranks of HMIC.

The Audit Commission is not alone: upon appointment to the Commission for Racial Equality, Sir Trevor Philips threatened to take legal action under the Race Relations Act against the police for their disproportionate use of stop and search against non-white people. However, in 2009 Sir Trevor (now chairman of the successor body, the Commission for Racial Equality and Human Rights) controversially expunged the taint of 'institutional racism' from the police entirely, despite racial disproportionality in stop and search *increasing* in the interim.

In 2003, a serving Commissioner of the Met. and his predecessor were prosecuted by the Health and Safety Executive after one officer fell through a roof to his death during the attempted arrest of a burglar in 1999 and shortly afterwards another officer fell through a roof, but survived. However, the application of Health and Safety legislation to the police has resulted in officers in public-order operations being obliged to don protective equipment that many commentators consider unnecessarily aggressive.

Public consultation is also a means through which the police may be influenced. Under section 106 of the Police and Criminal Evidence Act, the police are obliged to hold regular public meetings at which to explain police policy and other general matters – not specific arrests or operations. Heralded as an opportunity to hold the police to account, they became forums in which middle-aged and middle-class people took the opportunity to complain about minor nuisances, such as dogs fouling footpaths, and tended to fall into disrepute. More effective has been the informal growth of Independent Advisory Groups following the model of such a group to advise the Metropolitan Police on race relations after the Macpherson Report. Sometimes they represent particular sections of the population, while on others (such as the HMIC report into the policing of the G20 protests) they are selected for their specialist knowledge of subjects related to the content of a report.

In sum, the police are now pulled in various and often contradictory directions by influential external people and organisations, sometimes responding to specific events. The Police Federation persistently bemoans the absence of a Royal Commission to resolve what the police should do and how they should do it. The unpalatable truth is that policing is so central to the activity of the state that, as society has become more democratic, so there will be a popular clamour for the police to revise policy in favour of the chosen priorities of those who are making the demands. As an aspiring police officer you will need to brace yourself for a bumpy ride!

What does this mean for you?

What does all this mean for you embarking upon a policing career? It means that you will spend your life in a spotlight. There will be a host of regulators, commentators and policy makers proverbially looking over your shoulder. They will not judge you solely by whether you apply the law correctly, but by whether you have acted in a fully professional way, for instance in the way that you and your colleagues treat witnesses to murder.

CASE STUDY

Macpherson Inquiry's view of how the police treated witnesses

Duwayne Brooks was Stephen Lawrence's companion on the night Stephen was murdered:

5.10 We have to conclude that no officer dealt properly at the scene with Mr Brooks. His first contact was probably with Police Constable Linda Bethel. She described Mr Brooks as being 'very agitated'. Police Constable Joanne Smith said that he was 'jumping up and down and being very aggressive'. Police Constable Anthony Gleason said that Mr Brooks was 'Highly excitable. Virtually uncontrollable'. Considering what Mr Brooks had seen and been involved in, none of that should have been surprising. Furthermore, Mr Brooks was justifiably frustrated and angry, because he saw the arrival of the police as no substitute for the non-arrival of the ambulance, and to his mind the police seemed more interested in questioning him than in tending to Stephen.

5.11 Yet there is no evidence that any officer tried properly to understand that this was so, and that Mr Brooks needed close, careful and sensitive treatment. Furthermore, even if it was difficult at first to gain a coherent story from him the officers failed to concentrate upon Mr Brooks and to follow up energetically the information which he gave them. Nobody suggested that he should be used in searches of the area, although he knew where the assailants had last been seen. Nobody appears properly to have tried to calm him, or to accept that what he said was true. To that must be added the failure of Inspector Steven Groves, the only senior officer present before the ambulance came, to try to find out from Mr Brooks what had happened. He, and others, appear to have assumed that there had been a fight. Only later did they take some steps to follow up the sparse information which they had gleaned. Who can tell whether proper concern and respect for Mr Brooks' condition and status as a victim might not have helped to lead to evidence should he have been used in a properly coordinated search of the estate?

5.12 We are driven to the conclusion that Mr Brooks was stereotyped as a young black man exhibiting unpleasant hostility and agitation, who could not be expected to help, and whose condition and status simply did not need further examination or understanding. We believe that Mr Brooks' colour and such stereotyping played their part in the collective failure of those involved to treat him properly and according to his needs.

5.13 The ambulance men understandably would not allow Mr Brooks into the ambulance. PC Smith took him by car to the hospital, where she dropped him off at the entrance. At about 23:30 he was seen by PC Gleason, who recorded in his notebook a statement which was of great importance, since it was the first account recorded, and it contained at least one reasonable description of one of the attackers, including the information that the attacker had light brown hair. PC Smith found Mr Brooks to have been 'irate and aggressive'. She said that he used strong language saying 'Who called you fucking cunts anyway, pigs . . . I only called the fucking ambulance.' These things may well have been said. Perhaps they account for the fact that Mr Brooks was left to go into the hospital unaccompanied. Thereafter, apart from the contact with PC Gleason, which lasted until 23:57, when Mr Brooks signed his name in PC Gleason's notebook, nobody, and in particular no police officer, at any time treated him properly as a victim. He was left on his own, and eventually was told that he could not leave. Acting Inspector Ian Little told him to wait either in the hospital or in the police car. Mr Brooks did not want to be in the hospital, so he sat in the car. This treatment of Mr Brooks at the hospital is plainly subject to severe criticism. The support of a victim in such circumstances is essential. Mr Brooks was simply treated as a potential witness, and inadequately treated at that. We are convinced that the conclusion set out in Paragraph 5.12 must also apply to the treatment of Mr Brooks at the hospital.

(Source: Macpherson of Cluny, 1999)

As an aspiring professional police officer, all the matters discussed above will have a direct bearing on you and, later in your service, on those you command. Being professional means being accountable, because professionals know why they take particular courses of action. They are as liable to mistakes as any one – to err is human – but they would be able to identify the errors they made. What was so astounding about the Macpherson Inquiry was how a long line of police officers of all ranks appeared to enter the witness box without a moment's prior reflection on why and how things were done. The naivety shown by one officer after another was simply astonishing. For a professional police officer accountability should hold no terrors, because it is all part of what it is to be professional.

The spotlight dims only a little when police officers are off duty. Of course, as a holder of the 'office of constable' you will never truly be 'off duty', for your mandate is to preserve the Queen's Peace whenever or wherever it may be threatened. Beyond that, you will be judged by your conduct in all spheres of life; being a police officer is to be a public figure. Neighbours will come to learn that you are a police officer and they may turn to you for advice in all kinds of difficulty. You may find yourself as among the preferred chairmen of local civic societies. Equally, neighbours will expect your family life to be beyond reproach: a heated family row will be greeted with '. . . and him/her a copper too!'; and misbehaving children will elicit similar remarks. Friends will enjoy stories from the dark side of policing – police officers make good raconteurs – but you should never drop your guard and indulge in fanciful bragging that might come home to haunt you.

Remember that one of the most cataclysmic events in recent police history was the Macpherson Inquiry conclusion that the police were 'institutionally racist'. That did not rest on any clear evidence that anyone involved in the investigation of the murder of Stephen Lawrence had done anything egregiously racist. It rested on allegations from fellow officers, members of the National Black Police Association, who reported to the Inquiry the current of racist language that flowed through police canteens and other 'backstage' areas. The Inquiry needed to look no further for an explanation as to why non-white people were stopped and searched disproportionately. It was canteen banter that brought the police in this country into utter public discredit.

C H A P T E R   S U M M A R Y

In this chapter we have emphasised how policing tempts officers to stray into wrongdoing. It does so routinely through the proper exercise of discretion and the gap between experienced reality and the necessities of legality. All police officers teeter on the edge of this slippery slope because of the fundamental nature of policing, which is that it requires officers to perform as a matter of duty actions that otherwise would be exceptional, exceptionable or downright illegal. If you recognise the nature of what you are doing, you can appreciate its dangers.

Because of the exceptional powers given to the police, the state is watchful about how they are used. The processes of accountability have been progressively strengthened and look likely to be strengthened further, since strengthening accountability is an inevitable reaction to scandal and policing is scandal-prone.

Not only are you as a police officer subject to scrutiny, so too is the police organisation corporately accountable. This shifts considerably over time and you should remain aware of this broader context. After all, when the Macpherson Report (1999) branded the Metropolitan Police 'institutionally racist', this had direct and dire implications for patrolling officers, who were greeted by the local youths with cries of 'racist! racist! racist!'. Also, as a professional police officer you need to be aware of how your chosen profession is viewed by influential external audiences.

FURTHER READING

An intellectually and morally challenging view of police wrongdoing can be found in Maurice Punch's *Police Corruption* (Cullompton: Willan, 2009). You might like to compare this thesis with the opinions of reviewers in a special issue of *Policing: a Journal of Policy and Practice* (forthcoming). Also be attentive to episodes of wrongdoing by the police – alleged and/or substantiated – such as the recent conviction of Commander Ali Dezaei. Look beyond the salacious headlines and try to identify how good people can do bad things. This is also the theme of Philip Zimbardo's recent book, *The Lucifer Effect* (London: Rider, 2009), which, while not limited to the police, clearly has significant implications for them.

REFERENCES

Audit Commission (1996) *Streetwise: Effective Police Patrol*. London: HMSO.

Brogden, M (1991) *On the Mersey Beat*. Oxford: Oxford University Press.

Choongh, S (1998) Policing the dross: a social disciplinary model of policing. *British Journal of Criminology*, 38(4): 623–34.

Corbett, C (2003) *Car Crime*. Cullompton: Willan.

Feldberg, M (1985) Gratuities, corruption, and the democratic ethos of policing: the case of the free cup of coffee, in Elliston, F and Feldberg, M (eds) *Moral Issues in Police Work*. Totowa, NJ: Rowman and Allanheld, pp267–76.

Gangoli, G and McCarry, M (2008) Criminalising forced marriage. *Criminal Justice Matters*, 74: 44–6.

Garland, D (2001) *The Culture of Control: Crime and Social Order in Contemporary Society*. Oxford: Oxford University Press.

Hadfield, P (2006) *Bar Wars: Contesting the Night in Contemporary British Cities*. Oxford: Oxford University Press.

Harfield, C (2006) SOCA: a paradigm shift in British policing. *British Journal of Criminology*, 46(4): 743–61.

Jefferson, T and Grimshaw, R (1984) *Controlling the Constable*. London: Frederick Muller/Cobden Trust.

Macpherson of Cluny, advised by Cook, T, Sentamu, T and Stone, R (1999) *The Stephen Lawrence Inquiry* (Cm 4262-I). London: HMSO.

Manning, P (1997) *Police Work: The Social Organization of Policing*. Prospect Heights, IL: Waveland.

Matza, D (1969) *Becoming Deviant*. Englewood Cliffs, NJ: Prentice Hall.

Morton, J (1993) *Bent Coppers: A Survey of Police Corruption*. London: Warner.

Punch, M (2009) *Police Corruption: Deviance, Accountability and Reform in Policing*. Cullompton: Willan.

Short, M (1992) *Lundy*. London: Grafton.

Tombs, J and Jagger, E (2006) Denying responsibility. *British Journal of Criminology*, 46(5): 803–21.

Weinberger, B (1995) *The Best Police in the World: An Oral History of English Policing from the 1930s to the 1960s*. Aldershot: Scolar.

Wright, A and Irving, B (1996) Value conflicts in policing: crisis into opportunity: making critical use of experience. *Policing and Society*, 6(3): 199–211.

Zimbardo, P G (2009) *The Lucifer Effect: How Good People Turn Evil*. London: Rider.

8 Police and policing

At the end of this chapter you should be able to:

- locate policing funded by the state within a wider framework of security provision that includes a plethora of state and private organisations;
- recognise the role of civilian staff in the police organisation and acknowledge the contribution they make to the achievements of the police;
- appreciate the opportunities and challenges of working in partnership with other agencies.

Introduction

In this chapter we will distinguish policing from security and will identify various types of security personnel: official, semi-official and private. We will also explain the vital contribution of general social control to the achievement of social order and examine the dangers of vigilantism. In exploring the opportunities for partnership with these and other agencies for improving the quality of life for local people, we will also stress the importance of social cohesion.

Policing and security

It has become academically fashionable to distinguish the *activity* of 'policing' from the existence of 'public police' on the not unreasonable grounds that there is far more policing done by non-public police than by those whom we normally think of as the police. In this chapter we will explore the notion that policing is, at the very least, embedded within a wider spectrum of activities performed by many actors that can become partners to enhance the quality of life of those who live, work and visit an area.

Extended police family: PCSOs

The most obvious candidates to be embraced by an inclusive definition of policing is that of the 'extended police family' (to use the description employed by the former Metropolitan Police Commissioner, Sir Ian Blair). In truth, this is not a particularly recent departure; on the contrary, there is a long tradition of civilianisation, as it was once known. Long ago police officers abandoned vehicle parking enforcement to traffic wardens, who in the early days were often employed by the police, but who now tend to be employees of local authorities.

This was followed by various back-office functions being reallocated from police officers to civilian police staff: initially, the typing of reports and legal case papers passed from the single-fingered labours of officers to the efficiency of touch typists. Then police officers were removed from many control rooms as the latter took on the guise of call centres, which might just as well have been located in some developing country thousands of miles away for all the local knowledge they commanded. Civil staff then emerged into the front office of police stations, where most of the functions are clerical: taking reports from victims, recording details of drivers' licences and vehicle registrations, taking and storing found property and other such duties.

The growth and sophistication of forensic science has also meant that the role of Scenes of Crime Officers (or SOCOs) has passed progressively from regular officers to technically qualified civilian specialists. So the bad news is that anyone imagining that they will be the next Gil Grissom of *CSI* fame had better think again!

The latest, and possibly the most profound, development has been the introduction of Police Community Support Officers (PCSOs), who patrol the streets in uniform and perform many of the peacekeeping and order-maintenance duties previously the preserve of regular police officers. Even this is less novel than it might appear, for long before there was a professional police force Special Constables were sworn in to perform the full range of duties now thought to be the preserve of regular police officers. Gradually, the Special Constabulary emerged as a volunteer force with the legal powers of constables. Today, they receive extensive training, are regulated by the Performance, Conduct and Standards of Professional Behaviour regulations, and are subject to the Codes of Practice of the Police and Criminal Evidence Act 1984 (or PACE).

PCSOs have rather fewer powers than their Special Constabulary equivalents, which is a nice irony, given that PCSOs are, at least, full-time employees of police organisations, but such is the lumpiness of developments compelled by expediency. The expediency in this case was the paradox that, on the one hand, PACE imposed so many onerous responsibilities on regular police officers that training them became a major expenditure; while, on the other hand, most police work – and that most highly regarded by the public – requires little training. Why train officers to deal with the interrogation of a master criminal, when their daily routine was to walk unaided around housing estates?

The danger is that we are sleepwalking towards a gendarmerie model of policing, where PCSOs perform the non-confrontational role of the beat bobby and summon the heavy mob when circumstances dictate. The description of this as a 'gendarmerie model' is a little unfair to the French Gendarmerie, which paradoxically occupies in France the position and affection bestowed on the bobby on the beat in Britain. The use of the phrase 'gendarmerie model' has more to do with the historical animosity shown towards all things French by the British, who wrongly equate the Gendarmerie with heavy-handedness, just because the latter is a paramilitary force accountable to the Ministry of Defence, rather than the civilian Ministry of the Interior. The lesson is to beware of ill-informed comparisons!

However, the lesson is clear that, even within the police organisation, many duties that previously were restricted to serving officers have over the past half century been reallocated to civil staff.

Official and semi-official investigative and security agencies

In addition to the police, there is a host of other investigative and security organisations serving national and local government. The Security Service (widely known as 'MI5') deals with the most serious threats to the British state: countering espionage by the agents of actual and potential enemies; or preventing terrorist attacks by Al Qaeda-inspired terrorists. The Serious Organised Crime Agency (SOCA) does what it says on the letterhead, and investigates serious frauds, money laundering and trafficking in drugs, firearms and people. However, it is not a police agency and its personnel are only granted 'warranted powers' as and when necessary. HM Revenue and Customs investigates tax evasion by individuals and companies, and is granted wide-ranging powers of access to private property and documents. The UK Border Agency is not only responsible for monitoring and validating passports at ports of entry, but also investigates such serious organised crimes as people-trafficking.

There are also various police organisations that lie beyond those recognised by the Home Office, but which have constabulary powers. The British Transport Police claims that its pedigree can be traced to 1826 (three years before the Metropolitan Police was created). It polices the rail network, including tracks, sidings and stations, as well as the London Underground and various provincial local rail systems. The Civil Nuclear Constabulary has the distinction of being one of the only two permanently armed police forces in the country, the other being the Ministry of Defence Police, all of whom are trained in the use of firearms, which are carried by three-quarters of them at any one time. They are quite different from the Military Police, who are also routinely armed, but who are integrated into the armed forces and operate as such in the UK and abroad.

The Fire Service has its own investigation branch, which uses sophisticated techniques to identify the cause and location of suspicious fires and plays a vital role in the discovery of arson. The Royal Mail also possesses its own investigation branch, which examines various abuses of the mail service. The BBC, likewise, is empowered to detect and bring prosecutions against those who evade the television licence. The Environment Agency and local authorities maintain enforcement officers who detect, investigate and prosecute those who breach laws designed to keep the environment safe from pollution and other threats. Similar arrangements apply to health, where the central government's Health Protection Agency is supplemented by local Environmental Health Officers, who enforce standards of hygiene in food outlets and investigate episodes of food poisoning that can imperil the

97

lives of dozens of people. To these must be added Trading Standards Officers, who, among other things, investigate rogue traders who deceive householders out of considerable sums of money by unnecessarily repairing non-existent problems.

In addition to all these various agencies, there are semi-official investigators acting on behalf of the National Society for the Protection of Children, who investigate suspected child abuse; and the Royal Society for the Protection of Animals, which investigates serious cases involving organised dogfighting and much else besides.

Private security

By the most conservative estimates, the private security and guarding sector of the national workforce in Britain is more than double that of the public police. Consider what they do: they guard private property such as factories and warehouses (often containing valuable items), as well as shopping malls and places of entertainment. Many operate CCTV surveillance cameras and can effectively direct police officers to an incident or even organise the containment of an area to prevent the escape of a wanted person. On occasion, this can become legally problematic: for instance, in research on stop and search, Waddington et al. (2004) incidentally discovered that, in some circumstances, police officers stopped and searched people suspected by a civilian CCTV operator of committing an offence, without first-hand reason to suspect the person themselves.

Some private security operatives act as investigators, such as store detectives, who patrol self-service areas looking for those who attempt to avoid paying for goods, or forensic accountants, who scrutinise financial transactions for evidence of wrongdoing by clients and members of staff who might jeopardise the integrity of the financial institutions that employ them.

Journalism is also a powerful means of enforcing not only the law, but also standards of propriety. This was vividly brought to public attention in 2009, when the *Daily Telegraph* published details of expenses and allowances claimed by Members of Parliament that sparked public outrage, the premature termination of several political careers, and the criminal investigation of some MPs. Undercover journalists have penetrated political extremist organisations and serious organised criminal networks and have thereby prompted official action by the authorities.

Sometimes, the activities of journalists can be directed at those same authorities, as it was most notably when Mark Daley 'joined' the police and covertly recorded offensive racist talk among fellow recruits, which was broadcast as *The Secret Policeman* and was followed by the resignation or dismissal of those exposed and heaped further discredit on the police as a whole.

The degree of intrusion into individual privacy by journalists and photographers can also become a problem in its own right. For instance, journalists often rely upon members of various bodies leaking embarrassing or incriminating information, which might prompt a police investigation into how the information was leaked and by whom, with possibly severe consequences for those concerned. Often, the consequences of public disclosure of wrongdoing extends well beyond the criminal law, and adversely affects the lives of those disclosed, who may be dismissed from jobs and find further employment difficult; marriages and other relationships may collapse, and some have committed suicide in the wake of public revelations.

PRACTICAL TASK

Find your own enforcement agency

Using the internet, find as many non-police investigation and enforcement agencies or operatives in the UK as you can.

- *What powers do they have?*
- *What do they investigate and how?*

Social control

The above description of official, semi-official and private security only skims the surface of all the agencies and organisations, both public and private, that guard against law-breaking, enforce criminal laws and investigate suspected wrongdoing. However, all these organised bodies and individuals form only a small and rather ineffectual source of crime prevention and the maintenance of order.

Routine activity theory (Crawford, 2007) draws attention to how the way in which one leads one's personal life can facilitate or impede the commission of crime. For instance, the most prevalent time for burglaries to be committed is in the period between lunchtime and late afternoon, when parents tend to leave their homes unattended to collect children from school. Conversely, where property is easily overlooked by neighbours, burglaries are less likely to occur.

The presence or absence of capable guardians also has an influence on criminal activity; this embraces not only the police and other overtly security-oriented personnel, but many more people whose role is only incidentally concerned with crime and disorder. Figures such as park keepers, bus conductors and cinema usherettes, who once dispensed a variety of services to the public, also felt empowered to intervene early to quell behaviour that looked as though it might get out of hand. Unfortunately, many of these public servants have been sacrificed on the altar of efficiency.

Sociologists have long pointed out that social control is best achieved through the myriad groups and networks to which people belong. It is no accident that crime is most abundant where social and cultural capital is least in evidence. Social capital means the social networks upon whom one can draw for help and support when it becomes necessary. Cultural capital is the stock of knowledge that is available to a person, whether that is held in their own memory, or by members of the network, or on bookshelves, or on the internet. The importance of *what* and *who* one knows cannot easily be exaggerated, but this comes at a price, which is that one must behave in ways that encourage access to networks and stores of cultural knowledge. Making oneself acceptable to others involves submitting one's inclinations to the standards and norms that others expect or demand.

Sociologists have long been aware that gossip and ridicule are far more potent sources of control than rules and laws. Consider the impact that peer groups are thought to have upon the behaviour of those who belong to them: a young person who mixes with 'the wrong sort' might be tempted into substance abuse and other forms of criminality, whereas this is unlikely to be encouraged among student members of the Christian Union. Criminologists call this 'differential association', because whom one affiliates with is a selective process, although not one in which people are free to choose: if public housing is concentrated in vast estates with few facilities to entertain those who are condemned to live there, the chances are that the young residents of the estate will mix with each other, absorbing standards and norms of conduct that may lead them into conflict with police and other official agents of control (see Bottoms and Wiles (2002) for a discussion of the many ways in which the physical environment encourages or deters criminality).

CASE STUDY

Vigilantism and private or informal security

What is the difference between vigilantes and private or informal security measures? This is not an abstract question, because in dealing with the plethora of people, groups and organisations that exert social control or are employed to provide security, the issue of how much coercion they should use recurs. Private security firms 'do what it says on the can' – they provide security for private interests, that is, those who pay them. Wakefield (2003) found that, in three separate and very different locations, private security personnel were subordinate to the interests of their employers. Hence, types of people the management of malls or arts complexes did not wish to attract were simply excluded at the entrances or ejected if they penetrated very far.

There is no right to venture into private premises; the owners are perfectly entitled to decide who should or should not do so, and they employ 'muscle' to implement this policy. How much muscle should be used to eject those who are unwanted? This is an issue that is acutely encountered in the context of the night-time economy, when bouncers (now dignified as door supervisors and licensed by the Security Industries Association) implement the admission policies of pubs and clubs. Ejecting alcohol-fuelled young men is a recipe for violence and sometimes bouncers exceed the limits of using reasonable force.

Informally, too, people can go too far while informally enforcing codes of conduct. The Balsall Heath district of Birmingham has long had a reputation as a red-light area, and it has also increasingly played host to Muslim families for whom prostitution is an anathema. What began as community policing by individuals and groups informally patrolling the neighbourhood and taking the registration numbers of cars thought to be kerb-crawling, degenerated into intimidation and, sometimes, violence (Sharp et al., 2008).

The state took responsibility for the enforcement of criminal laws, not only to suppress criminal behaviour more effectively, but also to gain control of popular justice.

Formalisation of control

A debate rages within academic criminology about whether these developments have led to ever-increasing levels of control. This is not just in academic circles either – as we noted in an earlier chapter, the Information Commissioner, Richard Thomas, who is responsible for overseeing and occasionally adjudicating on issues of intrusion into personal privacy, has referred to the British 'sleepwalking into a "surveillance society"'. Conversely, one can point to the erosion of informal methods of social control in a world where people prefer to retreat behind their front doors.

We tend to align ourselves with the position of Trevor Jones and Tim Newburn (2002), who argue that the major shift has been towards the formalisation of social control. People occupying positions in society that commanded respect that empowered them to intervene to prevent or quell minor delinquencies, or who performed duties that incidentally involved maintaining order, have increasingly been replaced by officials (whether publicly or privately employed) whose principal function it is to ensure security.

This is not without its costs. Obviously, there is a substantial financial cost in employing a security guard to patrol a shopping area where once shopkeepers felt able to tell youngsters committing a nuisance to 'clear off'. There is also a potential cost to the criminal justice system, for when youngsters come to the attention of security guards they are more likely to be dealt with formally, which may entail being dealt with by the police (possibly by way of a formal caution). Hence, what was once dismissed as 'kids' stuff' can now find its way into formal records that might be used to authorise stronger sanctions.

Partnerships

There is an important lesson for those aspiring to become police officers: it is to appreciate how far effective policing is enmeshed in this complex web of capable guardians, informal networks, private security, official and semi-official law-enforcement bodies, and the growing corps of police staff. Regarded positively, this amounts to a huge network of people and agencies, all with a vested interest in keeping the peace. The police are not alone in dealing with the often difficult and seemingly intractable problems that are brought to their attention.

Consider for instance social housing, provided at rents that people on low incomes can afford. Occasionally, one finds in such housing areas anti-social individuals, families and groups who create misery for those among whom they live. These anti-social people may commit offences, but often they are so legally petty and sometimes so very difficult to prove as to effectively preclude using a criminal justice remedy. However, their actions are also very likely to constitute a breach of the tenancy agreements that such people have entered into with their landlords. The threat of losing their homes is likely to prove a far more persuasive influence over their behaviour than the remote prospect of being convicted of a minor public order offence. Consulting colleagues in the housing association or local authority about the remedy for a common problem mobilises resources that can be effectively deployed to change behaviour and improve the quality of life for others.

This is an example of partnership working – collaborating with as many as possible of those in the complex array of people and agencies mentioned above (and many more that were not) to find constructive ways of resolving local problems. Of course, the criminal justice sanction might be the preferred response to some problems, but the important point to remember is that it is not the *only* means at the disposal of the police.

Problem-oriented policing

Problem-oriented policing (POP) cautions police officers not to confuse ends and the means of achieving them. Its exponents argue that, in order to address problems, they must be:

- *identified*, by a process of *actively searching* for them; this might mean conducting a survey in an area to discover what residents, workers and visitors believe are the problems, and when and where they occur;

- *analysed*, by accumulating relevant knowledge and diagnosing the nature and source of the problem;

- *given a carefully tailored response*;

- *evaluated* and amended as necessary.

Evidence from a range of rigorously evaluated POP projects in different countries (Weisburd et al., 2008) – including a major evaluation conducted by the Home Office (Tuffin et al., 2006) – concluded that POP is far superior to traditional methods of policing. It has a modest impact on crime and disorder, but, perhaps more importantly, it garners public support. The reason is obvious: the public realise that the police are doing something serious about the problems that the public experience in their daily lives. In the British study, it was clear that the *process* of consulting with the public and finding inventive ways of dealing with problems was far more influential in raising levels of satisfaction and approval than were the *outcomes*. Being seen to recognise the importance of problems to the public and *try* to do something about them reaps its own reward.

However, POP is a demanding taskmaster. It is far easier to speed to a reported problem, 'blues and twos', and arrive just too late to capture the bad guys, than it is to take one's time to examine the problem in all its manifestations, collaborate and consult with as many others as the search for a remedy requires, evaluate it and make whatever adjustments are necessary. Yet, response policing rarely makes much difference to the quality of life of the public, whereas a carefully considered mobilisation of all the resources that may be employed in arriving at a resolution can pay handsome dividends.

It is important to be realistic and recognise that not everything can be achieved at once. Although it is not part of the POP creed, we would advise aspiring professional police officers to also *clearly prioritise* problems and address them in series. It is also necessary to be realistic: many of the problems that come to the attention of the police have their origins in deep personal and social issues over which the police (even in collaboration with others) can exercise only marginal influence. However, amelioration, rather than solution, is still a worthwhile goal.

Collaboration

Partnership working is likely to prove more effective than alternatives, but it, too, is no bed of roses. Partners inevitably have different and often divergent agendas: they may subscribe to various values; they may perceive and interpret 'the problem' differently; they may be drawn to certain kinds of solutions (as indeed are police officers drawn to criminal justice sanctions); and they may make different appraisals of the success or otherwise of a particular course of action.

For instance, police found themselves repeatedly being called to the same address in answer to suspected intruders in the early hours of the morning. On arrival, they found that it was an elderly and confused person living alone, who slept irregularly and awoke in the early hours of the morning frightened and bemused. The police suspected that the person needed medical help and possibly 24-hour care. However, they found that consultation with medical practitioners was severely impeded by the adherence of medics to 'medical confidentiality' (Irving and Dixon, 2002).

CASE STUDY

Partners and alcohol

There is a darker side to this, for the agendas of others may not be at all high-minded (as in the case of medical confidentiality). Private businesses must pursue commercial interests in order to remain viable, and local authorities must maintain commercially vibrant town centres to sustain their tax base, which enables them to continue providing public services. In the early 1990s, this became an unholy alliance, for, as the banks and building societies vacated the High Street, large pub chains saw an opportunity to extend their businesses by occupying these buildings and creating what we now call the '24-hour economy'. They negotiated their way around restrictions on the sale of drink late into the night, but needed the permission of magistrates (acting as licensing justices) to occupy former High Street banks and similar buildings. This tested the partnerships that police were trying to build with local authorities and commercial interests, because the police foretold what would happen if pubs and clubs were concentrated in limited areas (such as a single street) – there would be alcohol-fuelled violence and disorder. The police were unable to stop the 24-hour economy juggernaut from transforming town and city centres and it was a difficult time for partnerships (Hadfield, 2006).

Now liquor and entertainment licences are issued by local authorities, not magistrates, which arguably reinforces the potential for conflict between them and the police (Maguire and Nettleton, 2003).

Collaboration is, therefore, an exercise in tactfulness: persuading, negotiating, building trust and so forth. The good news is that other professionals often defer to the authority of the police. Indeed, one of the problems for officers in collaborative work is avoiding having all the responsibility heaped on their shoulders! Worthwhile collaboration often requires the consumption of vast quantities of tea and coffee, but that is a far more potent weapon than any other in the armoury of the police.

Cohesion

Ultimately, the goal for securing order and security is to build social cohesion in areas in which social and cultural capital are absent or lacking. This is undoubtedly a daunting task that requires the mobilisation of a vast array of public and private agencies and organisations. It is tempting for those who lack social and cultural capital to become dependent upon those who seek to help them, but dependency is often part of the problem and rarely plays any part in the solution.

There are, however, precedents to be found in the most unlikely places. The toughest unit in the British Army is undoubtedly the Special Air Service (SAS), which in the 1970s fought two more or less secret wars against insurgents trying to overthrow the Sultan of Oman (which borders the Persian Gulf and Arabian Sea on the south-east corner of the Saudi Arabian peninsula). They fought one war by confronting and defeating insurgents in battle, most famously at the fortress in Mirbat, where eight troopers defeated a force of 200 tribesmen. More remarkable was the defeat of the second insurgency in the high mountains of the north. The SAS hardly fired a shot in anger. Instead, they opened clinics in which to treat the ailments of the villagers and schools in which to educate the children. Once they had gained the trust of villagers, they equipped and taught them how to defend themselves against the insurgents. It took several years, but eventually the insurgency was defeated and Oman remained a stable and successful state. If the SAS can achieve so much in such testing conditions, bringing social cohesion to the crime and disorder-ridden areas of our cities should be within the grasp of local agencies led by the police!

What does this mean for you?

All this means that the job of the police is, and will remain, very different from how it is normally portrayed. The opportunities for chasing, capturing and securing the conviction of a master criminal are few and far between. But it is still possible to make a difference to the lives of ordinary people. Before social cohesion can be built, it is essential for order and security to be established.

This foundational role is clearly one for the police – some US projects describe this as 'weed and seed'. Weeding can be a pretty vigorous process and not one from which the police should shrink. But ground that has been weeded will quickly revert to its previous condition if the seeds are not sown and carefully nurtured. This too is a task for the police in collaboration with others. It is a task that calls for a mature approach and a miscellany of skills and knowledge. It is challenging and the likelihood of failure is ever present, but small gains can have enormous rewards for the quality of life of residents, workers and visitors to an area. It can also bring enormous job satisfaction.

When you've done one 'blue-light run' you have done them all; when you have smashed one door down the excitement at smashing others down wilts; when you have arrested yet another youthful offender for minor criminal offences, it is tempting to descend into cynicism; and when the criminal justice fails to deal with problems it was never designed to resolve, it is easy to abandon all hope. However, to see crime and disorder-ridden areas begin to be reclaimed – that is to appreciate the true meaning of policing!

C H A P T E R   S U M M A R Y

This chapter has focused on the security environment within which the police operate. This can be imagined as a series of concentric circles, in which the inner circle contains the 'extended police family', notably PCSOs, civilian support staff and the Special Constabulary. The next circle embraces an enormous array of official and semi-official investigative and security agencies, from MI5 and SOCA to inspectors for charities devoted to the protection of children and animals. Beyond those are all the private security operatives who guard locations or monitor CCTV, as well as journalists who sometimes expose wrongdoing. However, the biggest group are all those who engage in informal social control in the course of their daily lives, but who have an enormous impact on the behaviour of us all. The importance of all these groups for the police is that they offer fertile terrain for establishing partnerships. How one uses those partnerships is vitally important. Problem-oriented policing places emphasis on the police diagnosing the underlying problems that manifest themselves in crime and disorder, and arriving at carefully tailored ways of remedying them.

One implication of partnership is that the police, individually and corporately, need to get closer to people in the community – to discover what irks them and what resources can be mobilised to address those sources of discomfort. However, collaboration has its accompanying difficulties and these have been considered.

FURTHER READING

For a review of all the ways in which non-police agencies and individuals can and do contribute to security, Adam Crawford's review in the *Oxford Handbook of Criminology* (London: Centre for Criminology, 2007) is an excellent place to start and it offers further references for anyone wishing to pursue this issue further. Another essay in that same collection by Sir Antony Bottoms and Paul Wiles on 'Environmental criminology' draws attention to how the way in which the physical environment and its use can influence crime and disorder. Philip Hadfield's book, *Bar Wars* (Oxford: OUP, 2006), is an excellent case study of the influence that other actors may have on crime and disorder, and a cautionary tale about the agendas that potential partners may bring to the table. The official Home Office report on the impact of the National Reassurance Policing Programme, by Rachel Tuffin, Julia Morris and Alexis Poole (London: Home Office, 2006), is a fine illustration of how problem-oriented policing should be conducted.

ERENCES

Bottoms, A and Wiles, P (2002) Environmental criminology, in Maguire, M, Morgan, R and Reiner, R (eds) *The Oxford Handbook of Criminology*. Oxford: Oxford University Press, pp. 620–56.

Crawford, A (2007) Crime prevention and community safety, in Maguire, M, Morgan, R and Reiner, R (eds) *The Oxford Handbook of Criminology*. London: Centre for Criminology, Middlesex Polytechnic, pp866–909.

Hadfield, P (2006) *Bar Wars: Contesting the Night in Contemporary British Cities*. Oxford: Oxford University Press.

Irving, B and Dixon, W (2002) *'Hotspotting': Turning Police Theory into Practice in Thames Valley and Northumbria*. London: The Police Foundation.

Jones, T and Newburn, T (2002) The transformation of policing? Understanding current trends in policing systems. *British Journal of Criminology*, 42: 129–46.

Maguire, M and Nettleton, H (2003) *Reducing Alcohol-related Violence and Disorder: An Evaluation of the 'TASC' Project* (Home Office Research Study 265). London: Home Office Research, Development and Statistics Directorate.

Sharp, D, Atherton, S and Williams, K (2008) Civilian policing, legitimacy and vigilantism: findings from three case studies in England and Wales. *Policing and Society*, 18: 245–57.

Tuffin, R, Morris, J and Poole, A (2006) *An Evaluation of the Impact of the National Reassurance Policing Programme*. London: Home Office Research, Development and Statistics Directorate.

Waddington, P A J, Stenson, K and Don, D (2004) In proportion: race, and police stop and search. *British Journal of Criminology*, 44: 889–914.

Wakefield, A (2003) *Selling Security: The Private Policing of Public Space*. Cullompton: Willan.

Weisburd, D, Telep, C W, Hinkle, J C and Eck, J E (2008) *The Effects of Problem-oriented Policing on Crime and Disorder*. Oslo: The Campbell Collaboration.

Index